BEST VEGAN BODYBUILDING

QUICK AND EASY PLANT BASED HIGH PROTEIN RECIPES. PLUS A 7 DAYS MEAL PLAN TO GET STARTED

2

Table of Contents

INTRODUCTION

Veganism is the tradition of abstaining from using animal products, especially in diet, along with a related philosophy that interrupts the product status of animals. A follower of the doctrine is referred to as a vegetarian diet. Distinctions can be made between a number of types of veganism. Dietary vegans (known as "strict vegetarians") refrain from consuming beef, eggs, dairy goods, and some other animal-derived substances. An ethical dish (also called a "strict vegetarian") is someone who not only carries a vegetarian diet but expands the doctrine into different areas of their own lives, also opposes the use of animals for any use. Another word is "environmental veganism", which describes the avoidance of animal products on the assumption that the industrial farming of animals is environmentally harmful and unsustainable.

The Term "vegetarian" was in use since approximately 1839 to refer to that which was formerly described as a vegetable routine or diet. Its source is an intermittent substance of vegetable and the suffix -arian (in the sense of "supporter, believer" as in humanitarian).In the 1960s and 1970s, a vegetarian food motion emerged within the counterculture in the USA that focused on worries regarding diet, the environment, along with a distrust of food manufacturers, contributing to rising interest in gardening.

The subsequent decades saw study with several scientists and physicians in the USA, including doctors, who contended that diets based on animal fat and animal protein, like the Western routine diet, were more harmful to health. They created a collection of books which recommend vegetarian or vegetarian diets, which correlated meat consumption with ecological harm.

The Vegan diet became mainstream in the 2010s,particularly in the latter . The Economist announced 2019"the year of this vegan". The

European Parliament defined the significance of vegan for food labels in 2010, in force as of 2015. Chain restaurants started marking vegan items on their markets and menus enhanced their choice of food.

Plant-based meat earnings at the U.S have increased 37 percent in the previous couple of decades. By 2016, 49 percent of Americans were drinking plant milk, and 91% drank milk. In the UK, the plant milk market rose by 155% in two decades, from 36 million litres (63 million imperial pints) in 2011 to 92 million (162 million imperial pints) at 2013. There has been a 185% increase in brand new vegan goods between 2012 and 2016 in the united kingdom. In 2011, Europe's first vegetarian supermarkets seemed in Germany. In general, as of 2016, the biggest share of vegetarian customers worldwide now live in Asia Pacific with nine per cent of individuals following a vegetarian diet.

BASIC OF VEGAN DIET AND WHY GO VEGAN

Vegan and vegetarian diets seem to be one of the best food styles, but there's proof that a number of individuals have been ingesting a mostly wholesome or vegetarian diet for centuries. But it was not until 1944 that the word "vegan" was first coined. Basically, those who follow a vegetarian diet have chosen to eliminate all calcium-rich foods in their diet. Many select vegetarian clothes, household items and personal care items too. Most people who adopt a vegetarian diet do this for the perceived health benefits or to advocate for animal rights.

What Foods Make Up a Vegan Diet?

Vegan diets comprise of only foods that are fermented. This kind of diet includes vegetables, fruits, legumes, legumes, nuts and nut butters, fermented dairy options, fermented or noodle plant foods and whole grains. Vegan diets do not include animal foods such as legumes, dairy, poultry, meat or fish. They are also devoid of animal compounds like honey (produced by bees) and lesser-known animal-based ingredients such as whey, casein, lactose, egg white albumen, gelatin, carmine, shellac, animal-derived vitamin D3 and fish-derived omega-3 fatty acids.

Veganism and Health

The foods highlighted in a vegan diet are rich in many nutrients such as vitamins A, C, K and E, antioxidants, fiber and phytonutrients. Vegan diets are analyzed for their effect on human wellbeing. Below are a few highlights.

Health advantages of vegan diets also have been reported in observational research. 1 systematic overview of cross-sectional and prospective cohort studies reported reduced body mass index, total

8

cholesterol, LDL cholesterol (or "bad" cholesterol) and blood sugar levels in people following vegetarian or vegetarian diets when compared with omnivores. The outcomes of the research specific to individuals on a vegetarian diet signaled that this eating pattern decreased the total cancer risk by 15 percent. Though cross-sectional and cohort studies can't prove cause and effect (like a vegetarian diet induces health benefits), these findings support the results of RCTs, that are regarded as the gold standard of study and are intended to show that an intervention (after a vegetarian diet) results in a result (health benefits).

Most of this study has gained favorable outcomes. However, understanding the particular ramifications of vegetarian diets on health remains difficult due study with this eating pattern can be grouped with vegetarian or plant-based diets, each of which could consist of animal products.

Why Go Vegan

For Your wellbeing

Well-planned vegetarian diets follow healthy eating guidelines, also include each of the nutrients our bodies need. The British Dietetic Association and the American Academy of Nutrition and Dietetics realize They Are Appropriate for each age and stage of life. Some research has connected vegan diets with reduced blood pressure and cholesterol, and reduced rates of cardiovascular disease, type 2 diabetes and some kinds of cancer.

Going vegan is a good chance to find out more about cooking and nutrition, and increase your diet plan. Obtaining your nourishment from plant foods enables more space on your daily diet to get health-promoting choices like whole grains, nuts, fruit, seeds and veggies, that can be packed full of valuable fibre, minerals and vitamins.

For the animals

Preventing the misuse of animals isn't the only motive for becoming vegetarian, but for most it remains the crucial element in their decision to go vegan and keep vegan. Having psychological attachments with animals may form a part of the reason, although many think that all sentient animals have a right to existence and liberty. Specifics aside, preventing animal products is among the clearest means by which by which you can have a stand against animal cruelty and animal manipulation anywhere. A more thorough overview about why being vegetarian demonstrates accurate compassion for animals are available here.

For the environment

From recycling our household garbage to biking to work, we are all aware of methods to live a healthier life. Among the very best things an individual can do to reduce their carbon footprint is to prevent all animal products. This goes far past the issue of cow flatulence!

The creation of beef and other animal products puts a significant burden in the environment - from plants and water necessary to feed the animals, to the transportation and other procedures required from farm to fork. The huge quantity of grain feed necessary for meat production is a substantial contributor to deforestation, habitat loss and species extinction. In Brazil alone, the equivalent of 5.6 million acres of land is currently used to grow soya beans for animals in Europe. This property contributes to growing world malnutrition by forcing impoverished populations to develop cash crops for animal feed, instead of food to themselves. On the flip side, substantially lower amounts of water and crops have to maintain a vegetarian diet, which makes the switch to veganism among the simplest, most pleasurable and best approaches to decrease our impact on the surroundings.

For people

Just as veganism is your sustainable alternative when it comes to taking care of the world, plant-based dwelling can also be a more sustainable means of feeding your family. A vegetarian diet necessitates just 1 third of the property required to support a beef and meat diet. With increasing international water and food insecurity because of a plethora of socioeconomic and environmental troubles, there has never been a better time to embrace a more sustainable means of living. Preventing animal products isn't merely among the easiest ways a person can lessen the strain on meals in addition to some other sources, it is the easiest way to have a stand against ineffective food systems that disproportionately affects the poorest people around the world.

Muscle Growth And Veganism

As vegetarian diets become more popular than ever among customers, those who work out frequently might ask, "how can vegans build muscle with food that is wholesome?"

Building muscle for a vegan is all about easy lifestyle and dietary modifications; if you take building muscle badly in an expert level. By way of instance, if you are interested in working in bodybuilding, it is likely to be a winner in your area when avoiding animal products completely. For people who are only trying to tone up and preserve muscular, this is totally possible on a vegan diet too. To build muscle, you need nourishment, and contrary to what some think, it's totally feasible to get enough of it on a vegetarian diet. You can eat everything out of legumes such as lentils and legumes to soy-based foods and vegetarian meat products.

If you are attempting to build muscle, the narrative may be somewhat different. Nevertheless, you still do not have to fret too much about nutritional supplements when seeking to build muscle on a diet plan. "Vegan athletes' protein needs may vary from 0.36 to 0.86 g of protein per pound. Protein supplements aren't required to attain even the maximum degree of protein consumption.

After concerns about protein, the following thing some concern about when changing to a vegetarian diet is getting deficient in minerals and vitamins. Whilst everybody should be certain they're looking after their own body, those focusing on building muscle have to be particularly obsessed with their health and ensuring they're consuming all of the proper nutrients.

One of the most frequent deficiencies for people who follow a daily diet is B12, however, it is not just vegans who suffer with this. In fact, anybody who does not comply with a balanced diet is in danger of developing a vitamin B12 deficiency, indications of which include fatigue, depression, confusion, and equilibrium issues.

To eat enough B12, make certain you're eating foods like fortified cereals, nutritional supplements, and mushrooms. You might also beverage augmented esophageal milk, and if you want to, have a vegetarian nutritional supplement regularly. Another lack to know about is vitamin D, which may lead to muscle pain, in addition to depression and fatigue. Make sure you're carrying a multi-vitamin nutritional supplement, or eating beef fortified foods and getting enough sunlight to stop from becoming deficient in vitamin D.

It is possible to receive all the vitamins you need from foods that are fermented, but if you are trying hard to keep a balanced diet, then you can consult with a nutritionist or even employ a meal planner.

Can You Get Enough Calories To Build Muscle On A Vegan Diet?

As well as protein, getting sufficient calories is necessary to building muscle building, this can be a frequent problem for athletes and bodybuilders that transition to a vegetarian diet. But, beating the dilemma isn't overly hard, it's a case of incorporating healthy snacks in your diet plan.

Fruits and veggies are generally quite satisfying and low-calorie and consequently, it can be challenging for some to consume enough carbs, In this circumstance, vegan calorie-dense foods such as seeds, nuts, and peanuts ought to be inserted into smoothies or consumed as snacks. For bodybuilders that want to bulk up, attention and care when meal preparation goes a very long way. You might need to get creative with your diet programs, even if you're cutting weight and decrease food consumption. There are lots of 100% vegan bodybuilders... they establish it's possible.

Can You Be A Successful Bodybuilder On A Vegan Diet?

It is completely possible to become a successful bodybuilder whilst adhering to a vegetarian diet. Vegan bodybuilders have shown themselves efficiently on a vegetarian diet. Winning names in various distinct categories, they've excelled in conventional classes like classic bodybuilding in addition to figure, body and exercise. They have years of veganism between them. Proving they are able to obtain not just the protein but also essential minerals from plant sources, they've caused other competitions to reconsider their nourishment. Many have been given Professional Cards in big based bodybuilding federations.

14

Nimai Delgado grew up in Mississippi increased by Argentinian-immigrant Hare Krishna parents. He's been since birth, originally for spiritual reasons, and hasn't eaten meat.

Jehina Malik a born vegan was competing in bodybuilding because age 19 and is currently known as an accomplished competitor with an outstanding body, based on her" I never had been interested or wished to change my life style as animals in my opinion weren't supposed to be consumed, animals never been food alternative for me. What motivates me to keep being vegetarian is demonstrating to the world which you're able to be strong and healthy without consuming animals. I am living proof!"

Massimo Brunaccioni is an Italian bodybuilder who chose to go vegan for those animals around seven decades back. "nobody can state that vegans can't excel in bodybuilding, there are still a few who believe it inferior and discuss superior protein, not understanding the planet (and science) are going ahead."

What Should You Do, Eat, And Drink To Build Muscle On A Vegan Diet?

1. Consumer healthy calories

Have enough carbs on a plant-based diet can be difficult for fresh vegan bodybuilders, however it is vital that you attempt to eat the ideal amount. If you don't consume sufficient, you might begin to eliminate body mass since your body begins to use itself as a power supply, based on Bare Performance Nutrition.

To ensure you're getting enough calories, you need to look at choosing a vegetarian bodybuilding supplement, for example MyProtein. However, in addition, you must make certain you're consuming the correct foods. Pack in healthful proteins like nuts and quinoa, in

15

addition to fruits, like carrots and cauliflower. Nut butters such as peanut butter and almond butter also fantastic snacks in addition to fermented milk in smoothies. Soy milk will be the greatest in protein. You might even decide to snack on noodle jerky.

Contain vegan meats such as tempeh, tofu, seitan, and goods from manufacturers such as Gardein and beyond meat are great to maintain your routine meal turning. You can also look at cooking your meals in coconut oil to give it a calorie increase.

2. Eat Healthy Carbohydrates

Do not be fearful of carbs, they'll allow you to build muscle. But this does not mean you should gorge on snacks that are unhealthy. Adhere to low-glycemic carbohydrates, for example fiber-filled whole wheat bread and pasta. Eat oatmeal for breakfast, and attempt to package in beans and legumes such as chickpeas, lentils, legumes, and black beans to your foods daily.

3. Make sure you're getting Omega-3

Most Bodybuilders obtain their omega-3 -- aka polyunsaturated fatty acids which enable you to gain muscle and prevent injuries -- from bass, but it is completely feasible to also get it out of sources that are fermented. Walnuts are an especially excellent omega-3 supply, with much higher levels compared to salmon. The omega-3 fatty acid in carbohydrates is at another type than that in salmon. However, like salmon, when people eat omega-3 fatty acid in the kind of ALA they could also convert it into EPA and DHA. You do not require a salmon to convert it to you.

Flax seeds, Brussels sprouts, wild rice, chia Seeds, plant oils, fortified vegan milk, and algae oil can also be great sources of plant-based omega-3.

4. Eat Little but frequently

Eating small and often -- about six to eight small meals or large snacks -- will make it possible for you to keep a positive nitrogen balance on a vegetarian bodybuilding diet. It is vital that you get a steady stream of nutrients like protein, healthy fats, fats, and carbohydrates constantly entering your own body, the book notes. It provides that taking nutritional supplements can help to maintain this steady stream moving, but eating healthful plant-based snacks such as fruit, seeds, nuts, or pubs, is also crucial.

Perhaps not only does that help keep your body fueled and prepared for the next workout regimen, the novel continues, but in addition, it can help to improve your metabolism and cause you to burn fat quicker.

5. Maintain A food diary

Maintain track of everything you are eating, in order to understand which plant-based recipes and foods function for you. For busy times, perhaps it is a peanut butter and banana smoothie which really does the trick, or even a morning bowl of oatmeal. For days when you've got more time, experimentation with various recipes and note which ones were straightforward. Also notice that ones were more complex, as you might always prepare them in advance. You might also use your diary for supper prep, to plan out everything you are likely to consume during the week. This is a particularly great practice if you realize you have a busy week ahead of you, and you also do not wish to allow your balanced diet slide. If you are seriously interested in adhering to a vegetarian bodybuilding diet, then you must keep tabs on each and every bite and sip. Keeping a food diary is a wonderful choice, or there are lots of programs for monitoring your diet plan. Whenever you've got a food diary it's simple to mention how many protein and calories you have already consumed you can consume less

17

or more as needed. Additionally, it can help you to be conscious of your eating habits.

6. Supplement with vegan protein powder and bars

You may also supplement your diet with low-fat snacks such as rice protein shakes and bars. Sunwarrior creates a plant-based protein powder which may be Incorporated to a raw vegan diet and you made from peas and brown rice, Chocolate protein powder, which contains 20 g of protein per serving, utilizes A mix of pea, pumpkin seed, flax seed, chia seed, and quinoa protein. Vegan Athlete Brendan Brazier founded the plant-based protein manufacturer Vega, making A variety particularly designed to satisfy the nutritional requirements of athletes. It Additionally makes bars with titles that seem just like candy bars, such as Chocolate Peanut Butter and Mint Chocolate. Vegan protein snacks have become Increasingly common.

VEGAN FOODS AND BEST PROTEINS - MACRO AND MICRO NUTRIENTS …

Vegan diets are derived from grains and other seeds, legumes (especially beans), vegetables, fruits, leafy greens, and nuts). Veganism, is 'a method of living that attempts to exclude, so much as possible and practicable, all forms of exploitation of, and cruelty to, animals, such as food, clothes or any other function'. A vegetarian diet is totally free of all animal products, whether based from slaughter (for example, beef), or (like honey, egg and diary).

Protein sources

Vegans can struggle to find enough protein in their diets. Guys should eat roughly 55g of protein every day, girls 45g. Below are a few foods that are grated. Attempt to incorporate some protein at each meal.

Nuts and seeds are simple to throw into sandwiches or have to get a bite, and generally comprise 15--20g protein per 100g. There is also a developing array of nut butters to test. Peanut powder may be added to sauces or smoothies.

Beans and lentils may thicken soups, sauces, dips and bakes and have a tendency to comprise around 10--20g protein per 100g.

Soya products, where the best is kale, are rather low in fat and may be utilized in an assortment of means. Tofu comprises about 8g of protein per 100g. Soya milk and soya yoghurt can also be great sources of nourishment. Meatless products predicated on legumes (tofu), or wheat-based seitan are sources of plant protein, generally in the kind of vegetarian sausage, mince, and veggie burgers. Soy-based dishes are typical in vegan diets since soy is a protein resource. They're consumed most frequently in the shape of soy milk and tofu (bean curd), that can be soy milk blended with a coagulant. Tofu comes in many different textures, based on water content, company, moderate business and extra firm for stews and stir-fries to tender or silken for salad dressings, desserts and powders. Soy can be eaten in the kind of tempeh and fresh vegetable protein (TVP); also called textured soy protein (TSP), the latter is most frequently utilized in wheat noodles.

Wheat protein (seitan) and fermented foods (tempeh) are more moderate meat substitutes that are not as effective in flavor than kale but high in protein

Protein-fortified products abound, such as vegan balls. Look out for the sum of fat and sugar in them however, as protein isn't a byword for wellbeing, and also be conscious it is possible to consume an excessive amount of protein.

Magnesium sources

Since vegans do not consume milk, calcium needs to be utilized in products that are fortified. Some plants don't contain calcium but in comparatively low levels. Calcium-fortified tofu, soya yoghurt, soya milk, breakfast cereals, orange juice as well as breads are readily available.

Iron sources

A healthy and diverse vegan diet must include enough iron should you consume these foods frequently:

Beans, Peas and lentils

Tofu

Seeds and nuts

Dried fruit, like raisins, dates or apricots

Dark-green vegetables, like spinach, kale and broccoli

Wholegrain rice and wholemeal bread

Fruits and vegetables full of vitamin C, also that make the iron from plant-based foods bioavailable.

Omega-3 Sources

Omega-3 Fatty acids fall into 2 groups:

DHA and EPA: those long-chain omega-3 fats possess crucial advantages to brain growth and cardiovascular health and therefore are particularly important for young children and pregnant ladies. The body is able to create these from ALA, but less efficiently as though you eat them straight. Microalgae-based omega-3 nutritional supplements can be found as an alternate to nutritional supplements made out of fish oils.

ALA: This sort of omega-3 fat lies in a selection of vegetarian sources, such as chia seeds, ground flaxseed (linseed), rapeseed oil, walnuts, and hazelnuts, pecans and green leafy veggies. ALA can not be produced by the entire body, therefore it is very important to have enough from these types of sources.

Nutritional supplements

There are several vitamins and nutritional supplements which are better supplied as a supplement to your vegetarian diet. Check the label to be certain supplements include no gelatine or alternative animal-derived products.

Omega-3 (see above); it's hard to acquire sufficient omega-3 out of a vegetarian diet, however, vegetarian nutritional supplements are readily available.

Vitamin B12 is included to Many food items, such as yeast infections, non-dairy milks, and nutritional elements, but if you do not consume these foods frequently you should take a supplement

Iodine Amounts in food and therefore are changeable so that it's hard to learn how much you are getting out of meals. Obtaining a supplement will make certain you get sufficient.

Vitamin D is created by the human body from exposure to sun, however the sun is not powerful enough in the united kingdom through winter, so lots of men and women choose a vitamin D supplement during those months.

VEGAN FOODS

1. Legumes

In an attempt to exclude all forms of animal exploitation and cruelty, vegans avoid conventional sources of iron and protein like poultry, meat, eggs and fish.

Therefore, it is necessary to replace those animal products together with protein- and - iron-rich plant options, like legumes.

Beans, Peas and lentils are fantastic choices which include 10--20 g of protein a cup.

They are also excellent sources of fiber, including slowly digested carbohydrates such as iron, folate, manganese, zinc, antioxidants along with other antioxidant plant chemicals.

But, Legumes also have a fantastic number of antinutrients, which can lessen the absorption of the minerals.

For Example, iron absorption in crops is projected to be 50 percent lower than that from animal sources. In the same way, vegetarian diets appear to decrease zinc absorption by roughly 35 percent in contrast to those containing beef. It is beneficial to sprout, cook or jelqing beans well since these procedures can reduce the amount of antinutrients.

To Raise your absorption of zinc and iron from beans, you can also should prevent consuming them in precisely the exact same period as foods that are calcium-rich. Magnesium can interfere with their absorption should you have it in precisely the identical moment. By comparison, eating beans in conjunction with vitamin C-rich fruits and veggies can further boost the absorption of iron.

DRIED LEGUMES

Black eyed beans

White Kidney beans

Fava beans

Pinto Legumes

Kidney Legumes

Green Foods

Red Foods

French Foods

Split Peas, green and yellow

Adzuki Legumes

Navy Legumes

CANNED LEGUMES

Black Legumes

Kidney Legumes

White Kidney beans

Pinto Legumes

Black eyed peas

Lentils

2. Nuts, Nut Butters and Seeds

Nuts, their byproducts are a fantastic addition to almost any dish fridge or pantry. That is in part as a 1-oz (28-gram) serving of nuts or seeds comprises 5--12 g of protein.

This makes them a fantastic alternate to eponymous creature solutions. Additionally, seeds and nuts are excellent sources of iron, magnesium, fiber, selenium, magnesium and vitamin E. They also have a fantastic number of antioxidants as well as other beneficial plant chemicals.

Nuts and seeds can also be extremely versatile. They are sometimes consumed in their own, or labored to intriguing snacks like snacks, sandwiches and desserts. Cashew cheese is just one yummy choice. Favor nut butters which are natural instead of heavily processed. These are normally devoid of this petroleum, salt and sugar frequently added to family brand types.

- Sausage: walnuts, pecans, brazil nuts, cashews, hazelnuts, pine nuts, pistachios
- Seeds: hemp seeds, sunflower seeds, chia seeds, sesame seeds, flaxseeds, pumpkin seeds (pepitas)
- Nut butter: cashew butter, almond butter, peanut butter
- Seed butter: sunflower seed butter, tahini

3. Hemp, Chia Seeds and Flax

All these three seeds have particular nutrient profiles which have to be highlighted individually from the prior group. For starters, all three include larger quantities of protein compared to most other seeds.

26

One Ounce (28 g) of berry seeds contains 9 grams of total, readily digestible protein about 50 percent more protein than most other seeds. What is more, the omega-3 into omega-6 fatty acid percentage contained in hemp seeds is also deemed best for human wellbeing.

Research also proves that the fats present in seeds might be rather good at decreasing symptoms of premenstrual syndrome (PMS) and menopause. It might also decrease inflammation and enhance specific skin ailments .For their role, chia and flaxseeds are especially saturated in alpha-linolenic acid (ALA), an important omega-3 fatty acid that your body is able to partially convert to eicosapentaenoic acid (EPA) and docosahexaenoic acid (DHA). EPA and DHA play significant roles in the maturation and maintenance of the nervous apparatus. These long-chain fatty acids also appear to play valuable roles in pain, inflammation, depression and nervousness.

4. Tofu and Other Minimally Processed Meat Substitutes

Tofu and tempeh are processed meat substitutes manufactured from soybeans. Both comprise 16--19 g of protein each 3.5-oz (100-gram) percentage. They are also great sources of calcium and iron.

Tofu, generated in the pressing of soybean curds, is a favorite substitute for meats. It may be sautéed, weathered or broiled. It creates a great choice to eggs recipes like omelets, frittatas and quiches.

Tempeh consists of fermented soybeans. Its distinctive taste makes it a favorite substitute for fish, however, tempeh may likewise be utilized in various different dishes.

Tofu of all types

Tempeh

Edamame

Soy Protein

Soy milk

5. Calcium-Fortified Plant Milks and Yogurts

Vegans often eat smaller quantities of calcium daily than meat eaters, which might negatively influence their own bone health. This seems particularly true when calcium intake drops below 525 milligrams every day.

For this rationale, vegans should try to create calcium-fortified plant milks and plant life yogurts portion of their everyday menu. Individuals seeking to concurrently increase their protein consumption should elect to get milks and yogurts made of soy or berry. Rice, coconut, almond and oat milks are all lower-protein choices.

Calcium-fortified plant milks and yogurts are often additionally fortified with vitamin D, a nutrient which plays a significant part in the absorption of calcium. Some manufacturers also include vitamin B12 for their own products. Thus, vegans appearing to achieve their daily intakes of calcium, vitamin D and vitamin B12 throughout meals should be certain that you elect for products that are augmented. To maintain added sugars to a minimum, be certain that you pick unsweetened versions. .

- Coconut milk
- almond or cashew yogurt
- cashew cheese
- dairy-free milk like oat, rice, almond, soy, hemp, cashew or coconut

6. Seaweed

Seaweed is among those rare plant foods to feature DHA, an essential fatty acid which has many health advantages. Algae like spirulina and chlorella can also be great sources of protein.

2 Tbsp (30 ml) of them provide about 8 g of protein. Additionally, seaweed includes magnesium, magnesium, riboflavin, manganese, phosphorus, potassium and very good quantities of antioxidants. The nutrient iodine, specifically, plays essential roles on your metabolism and also at the role of the thyroid gland. The Reference Daily Intake (RDI) of potassium is 150 micrograms every day. Vegans can fulfill their needs by consuming a number of portions of seaweed each week.

That being mentioned, some sorts of seaweed (for instance, kelp) are very high in potassium, therefore shouldn't be consumed in considerable quantities.

7. Nutritional Yeast

Nutritional yeast is created of a deactivated breed of Saccharomyces cerevisiae yeast infection. It may be located in the kind of yellowish powders or powder in many grocery stores and health food shops. 1 ounce (28 g) comprises approximately 14 g of protein and 7 grams of fiber. Additionally, nutritional supplement is often fortified with magnesium, zinc, magnesium, manganese and B vitamins, including vitamin B12.

Therefore, Fortified nutritional supplement may be sensible means for vegans to achieve their everyday vitamin B12 guidelines. But, it is essential to be aware that vitamin B12 is light-sensitive and might degrade if purchased or saved in plastic bags. Non-fortified nutritional supplement shouldn't be relied upon as a source of vitamin B12.

8. Sprouted and Fermented Plant Foods

Even though rich in nutrition, many plant foods also include varying quantities of antinutrients. All these antinutrients may cut back your body's capacity to absorb the nutritional supplements that these foods include. Sprouting and fermenting are easy and time-tested procedures of decreasing the quantity of antinutrients utilized in a variety of foods. These methods increase the sum of valuable nutrients consumed from plant foods and may also improve their general protein quality. Interestingly, sprouting can also slightly lower the total amount of gluten found in certain grains. Fermented plant foods are all great sources of pancreatic cancer, which might help improve immune function and digestive health. They also include vitamin K2, which might promote dental and bone health in addition to help reduce the danger of cardiovascular disease and even cancer.

9. Whole Grains, Cereals and Pseudocereals

Whole Cereals, grains and polyunsaturated fats are all good sources of complex carbohydrates, fiber, calcium, and iron, in addition to B vitamins, magnesium, calcium, magnesium, selenium and zinc.

That Explained, some forms are more beneficial than others, particularly in regards to protein. As an example, the early grains spelt and teff include 10--11 g of protein a cooked cup (237 ml). That is a lot when compared with wheat and also rice. The noodle cereals amaranth and quinoa come at a close second with approximately 9 g of protein a cooked cup (237 ml). They're also a couple of the rare sources of protein inside this food category. Like most plant foods, whole grains and noodle cereals include varying amounts of antinutrients, which may restrict the absorption of valuable nutrients. Sprouting is helpful for decreasing these antinutrients.

As to get flours, I inventory quinoa bread and chickpea flour for sandwiches and utilize whole-wheat or fermented flour for baking.

Wrapped oats, steel-cut oats

Wild rice, brownish rice, along with other rice types

quinoa

farro

freekeh

millet

amaranth

teff

31

buckwheat

barley

Bakery: buns, tortillas, breads

Pasta: Quinoa pasta, brown rice, whole wheat pasta

Rice Cakes

Whole Grain flours: buckwheat flour, quinoa flour, whole wheat germ

10. Choline-Rich Foods

The nutrient choline is very important to the health of the liver, brain and nervous system.

Our bodies can create it, but just in tiny quantities. That is the reason why it's regarded as a vital nutrient you have to get from the diet plan. Choline could be found in Tiny quantities in a Vast Array of vegetables, fruits, nuts, legumes and grains

That said the plant foods together with the biggest levels include tofu, soymilk, broccoli, cauliflower and quinoa.

11. Fruits and berries

Some vegans rely heavily on meats and vegetarian junk food to substitute their preferred animal foods. Nonetheless, these kinds of foods tend to be highly processed and fat.

Fortunately, there are several means to change out your favorite foods with vitamin- and - mineral-rich fruits and veggies instead. As an example, mashed banana is a fantastic substitute for eggs in baking soda.

Banana ice cream is also a favorite substitute for dairy-based ice cream. Simply combine a frozen banana till it is smooth. Then you are able to add your favorite toppings.

Eggplant and mushrooms, particularly cremini or portobello are a terrific way to receive a meaty feel in vegetable kind. They are especially simple to grill.

Maybe astonishingly, jackfruit is a superb stand-in for meat from delectable dishes like stir-fries and sausage sandwiches.

Meanwhile, steak is a flexible addition to a lot of recipes, such as pizza crust. Vegans should also plan to maximize their consumption of iron and calcium-rich vegetables and fruits. Including leafy greens like bok choy, kale, spinach, watercress and leafy greens.

Turnip greens, broccoli, artichokes and blackcurrants are also excellent choices.

Processed Dairy Alternatives

We will talk about processed foods after in this book but if you are just starting out and want some milk alternatives that will help you transition, then you can think about things like:

vegan sour cream
vegan cream cheese
cheddar or mozzarella fashion churns
cheese Pieces
Chocolate soy or almond milk
Coconut creamer
Earth Balance butter

vegan ice cream

Herbs And Spices

Having a spoonful of dried spices and herbs can allow you to produce flavorful foods with no demand for excessive salt. That said, because you are going to be ingesting low-sodium, whole foods (instead of processed foods which contain excessive sodium), there is nothing wrong with having a fantastic excellent sea salt on the kitchen to taste your food. Sea salt is full of trace minerals and may be a very healthy addition to your daily diet.

The two fresh and dried spices and herbs are full of antioxidants and also have lots of anti-inflammatory and beneficial properties. My favorites are ginger, garlic, garlic, cilantro, basil, dill, cumin, cinnamon and coriander.

Adding herbs & spices into your food not just kicks up the taste but is also rather helpful to your wellbeing. A number of these seasonings arrive with tremendous anti-inflammatory and antioxidant capacities.

· Dried basil, new as necessary
· Dried bay leaves
· Celery seed
· Ground chili powder
· Red pepper flakes
· Cayenne pepper
· New chives
· Fresh or dried cilantro (coriander)
· cloves
· cumin
· Curry powder
· turmeric
· Fresh garlic, garlic powder
· New gingerroot, ground ginger

34

- Italian Taste
- ground thyme
- onion powder
- Dried peppermint
- Dried rosemary, refreshing as necessary
- Dried dill, fresh as necessary
- Dried lemon, fresh as necessary
- Black peppercorns
- Sea salt

Natural Sweeteners

Whether you use sweeteners on your own kitchen is left up to you. I utilize banana, dates, applesauce, coconut oil, maple syrup and stevia in my own kitchen. If you enjoy baking, you may use some of those sweeteners below to get an unrefined alternative to refined sugar.

- agave syrup
- coconut sugar
- maple syrup
- molasses
- stevia
- Organic cane sugar
- dates

Condiments

All these things are great for carrying the taste of those vegetables a notch up. I stock all these and use them frequently to make sauces, sauces and curries and taste all types of dishes.

· Coconut milk
· Red curry paste
· Green curry paste
· Soy sauce or fermented tamari
· miso paste
· mustard
· salsa
· organic ketchup
· Sweet chili sauce

Food Labelling

Food Labelling for pollutants must determine where egg or milk yolk are found, so check that on any foods that are processed.

Most wines, many spirits along with a few beers' are 'fined' (explained) or filtered with animal products like egg white or isinglass, that can be based on the swim bladder of a fish. Read the labels and then select beverages that say they're acceptable for vegetarians and vegans. The great thing is that there is a larger assortment of high-quality vegetarian beverages than in the past.

Mycoprotein (Quorn) is occasionally made out of small quantities of egg white, although a few Quorn products are vegetarian and therefore are currently clearly tagged.

Honey can become a vegetarian food. Vegan substitutes incorporate gold syrup, agave syrup or maple syrup.

Meat stocks may turn up in readymade soups, risottos and gravies.

Food Colouring E120 -- a few candy or beverages can be colored with cochineal, up the ground cubes of the cochineal beetle.

Whey and casein are berry fats which could be discovered in many processed foods like protein bars, breads, biscuits and crisps. The allergens part of this tag should flag up this.

Gelatine can be used in candies, especially those kinds and marshmallows. Occasionally gelatine is inserted to nutrient supplements in capsule type. You will find vegan versions readily available, so look around.

Pasta Can be produced with egg, if dried or fresh.

Foods to try out

Nutritional yeast seems less than attractive; however this deactivated yeast merchandise (also called 'nooch') gets the advantage of tasting really cheesy as well as gallop. It's also full of B vitamins and protein. Use it into vegan cheese sauces, baking soda, or as a garnish instead like Parmesan.

Aquafaba is a fancy term for the water enclosing tinned chickpeas. As it contains proteins in the chickpeas, it's the outstanding ability to maintain a foamy condition when refrigerated, which makes it a superb substitute for egg whites within beef meringues, mayonnaise and mousses. The effectiveness of various brands of chickpeas (along with other legumes) can differ.

Seitan is wheat protein that's derived from wheat germ (the protein ingredient of this flour). The gluten free is extracted out of wheat then processed to replicate meat. It comprises a whole lot of protein and contains a deep texture. It may be barbecued, shiny, roasted, stir-fried, deep-fried or cooked in almost any manner meat could be.

Macronutrient in vegan diet

So It is super easy to fulfill, or even surpass your nutrient needs on a vegetarian diet. There's not any magic powder, shake or pill only genuine, ALIVE, complete foods. To fully grasp how to attain and maintain a nutritious diet, firstly it's very important to comprehend the function of macronutrients & micronutrients in your system. The 3 macronutrients we need to flourish are carbs, protein and fats. Yes, we need all them and every macronutrient is equally as crucial as another.

Carbohydrates are our bodies main fuel supply; they're broken down to sugar and are liable for fueling ALL cellular capabilities. Evidently, regardless of the lousy wrap that carbs make, they have a vital place in our daily diet. Do not get me wrong, there are a few carbohydrates which don't evoke many health advantages apart from energy. Examples of them are likely what you're already believing! Highly processed foods such as sugary cakes, cereals, packed potato processors, sugar-sweetened beverages, processed sugars etc. This is just talking because these kinds of carbohydrates aren't within their entire food type and therefore are processed, hence losing a lot of their nourishment and most of all their fiber content. The great news is that there are loads of carbohydrates to include things like which are great gas sources as they're whole foods, minimally processed and also include fiber. Cases are:

Entire Sausage : buckwheat, rice, spelt, sorghum, amaranth, quinoa, teff, whole grain pasta and wholegrain sourdough bread.

Berries : No vegetable is a lousy vegetable clearly! Include all of them, starchy vegetables like corn, wheat, sweet potato and white curry comprise a increased carbohydrate material however have a useful place in our coconut dishes also!

38

Berries : Again, all sorts of fruit are excellent whole food sources of carbs.

Fat could be a very confusing issue Especially one of the community, so let us break it all down. Again, the fat is necessary for many functions in the human body. It helps with fat-soluble vitamin consumption (vitamin A, vitamin D, E and K) and is needed for healthy cell structure inside our own bodies like hair and skin ethics. Fat supplies energy, aids in preventing balance and signaling blood flow and mind growth. It's safe to say fat is superb significant, there are a couple of distinct kinds of fat; saturated fat, monounsaturated, polyunsaturated and trans fat.

AVOID Saturated and Trans fats. Saturated fat ought to be used sparingly because it can improve your cholesterol and so boost cardiovascular disease risk. Saturated fat is found in animal and animals bi-products e.g. dairy and meat. Fantastic news is to a vegetarian diet we do not eat these! Trans fats aren't something you may encounter to considerably if you're adhering to an entire food diet. It's found in processed foods such as margarines such as chips, biscuits and cakes etc. Aim to fully prevent this kind of fat because there aren't any nutritional advantages so keep your eye on your food labels when swallowing processed foods.

INCLUDE Monounsaturated fats, all these are fats that evoke very good health benefits like lowering LDL (bad) cholesterol and raising HDL (good) cholesterol.) Healthy sources include; eucalyptus, olive oil, avocado, and all sorts of seeds and nuts. Polyunsaturated fats (Omega 3 & 6) are fats that we will need to eat through our daily diet because our body can't make these fatty acids. Healthy sources include; tempeh, tofu, edamame beans, flaxseeds, walnuts, sunflower seeds, chia and also my personal favorite berry seeds.

39

Last but not least (Obviously, since we've verified that macronutrients are significant) let us discuss nourishment.

Protein: Could I start off by saying yes, then it's wholly feasible to find enough protein to your diet. In reality, all of the hype about protein is really silly, we do not require copious quantities of protein! While it is still quite significant, if we have a lot of it merely gets damaged (wasted) and breeds our own bodies blockers (kidneys). Back to its significant function, its vital for many bodily activities like transport throughout the entire body, cellular architecture and bodily functions, resistance and regulation processes such as digestion.

There Are twenty kinds of amino acids, that are the building blocks of the protein. Nine of that we are not able to create within the human body and consequently we will need to eat them inside our daily diet, these are known as essential amino acids. Fantastic news is that it is absolutely achievable to find these two amino acids in healthful foods!

Healthy Sources include ; tempeh, tofu and edamame beans. Legumes and lentils such as, black beans, broad beans, kidney beans, peas, lentils, legumes and chickpeas. Nuts like almonds, peanuts, pecans, brazil nuts, avocados, cashews and macadamias. Seeds like sesame, pumpkin seeds, buckwheat and berry seeds. Additionally, Most grains include protein and one especially great supply is quinoa. Last but not the least, green leafy vegetables contain good quantities of protein too.

Micronutrients To Look Out For

The vegan people had, but an inadequate intake of several vitamins, that might have a negative health impact. Compared to the findings, previous research studies, reporting consumption of vitamin A (retinol equivalents; RE) discovered greater consumption of Vitamin A in vegans compared to omnivores. But, it's hard to compare outcomes across research because the quantity of retinol and beta-carotene, where the vitamin A consumption is calculated, isn't presented. These conflicting results may be a result of various procedures of calculating vitamin A RE out of beta-carotene along with other carotenoids. The vegan consumption of retinol was quite low in the current study in contrast to previous studies . In the current research that the 2001 Institute of Medicine Interconversion of Vitamin A and vitamin Carotenoid Units has been implemented. Retinol is mainly found in animal products, why the finding in the current study looks plausible. Around half of those vegans didn't achieve the exact recommendations vitamin A containing the two intake from diet and nutritional supplements. Indicators of Vitamin A deficiency are night blindness, dry and scaly skin cancer, higher number of diseases in the lymph nodes, both the gut as well as the urinary tract and acute vitamin A deficiency has additionally been connected to cancer in these websites.

The vegans engaging in the current study Had a minimal intake of riboflavin and vitamin B12, which equates with previous findings. The significant food sources of riboflavin in Nordic diets include meat and milk products, which describe the minimal intake of the vitamin one of vegans. Recommended intake of riboflavin and vitamin B12, such as consumption from supplements, isn't attained by 29 and 31 vegans (of 70), respectively. Little attention was paid to the consequences of riboflavin deficiency on individual wellness. An in vitro study with duodenal biopsies revealed that riboflavin imbalance in mature individuals impairs proliferation of cells and thus could have consequences for digestive function and nutrient absorption. With no supplementation the reduced dietary intake of vitamin B12 one of vegans could improve threat of lipoic acid and polyneuropathy.

In 41 (of 70) vegans that the whole consumption of vitamin D did not fulfill the recommendations. The effect of inadequate intake of vitamin D is significantly reduced absorption of potassium and calcium, which might affect bone metabolism. What's more, it's been indicated that elevated vitamin D plasma immersion or vitamin D supplementation is associated with reduced risk of esophageal cancer,

41

cardiovascular disease and type 2 diabetes. The ingestion of vitamin D and Vitamin B12 one of vegans was low in the current study and it's lower than that which was observed in prior research.

In the current study, ingestion of dietary sodium one of vegans was reduced compared to overall population. Three studies have examined the salt content of a vegetarian diet two of which also revealed lower sodium consumption among vegans, whereas the next study found no distinction between a vegetarian diet and an omnivore diet. The minimal consumption of sodium at the vegan people in this study may be caused by a decrease consumption of processed foods, which normally contain high levels of sodium. The majority of the vegans (55 of 70) did not fulfill the recommendation for nutrient intake when adding intake in supplements. Just 1 study has investigated iodine ingestion in vegans reporting that an iodine intake from supplements and diet among vegans of just 50--70 percent of their dietary plan value.

In general, potassium and sodium intakes are hard to measure and the outcomes must be interpreted with care. Greater than half the vegans (24 of 70) attained the recommended intake of supplementation. No studies have examined selenium consumption in vegans. An inadequate consumption of potassium and selenium may possibly have adverse health effect like growth of goiter. Adequate nutrient intake is essential during life, however, particularly in youth and throughout pregnancy and breastfeeding.

Minerals and vitamins interact and are dependent upon adequate accessibility to one another so as to operate and contribute to make sure human wellbeing. Cases include vitamin A and zinc, each B-vitamin in addition to vitamin D and calcium. This highlights the value of sufficient intake of each individual mineral because, for example, an insufficient intake of vitamin A affects the purpose of zinc though this vitamin is consumed in adequate quantities as is true for those vegans in this research.

42

8 Key Nutrients To Add Within A Healthier Diet To Prevent Malnutrition

1. Iron

Red blood cells adore iron fortunately, liver and beef are not the sole sources of the vital mineral. Dried beans and legumes, lentils, improved cereals, whole-grains, dark leafy vegetables, and dried fruit (hi, raisins!) Are great sources of iron. Nevertheless, individuals who don't consume poultry, fish, or fish need nearly two times as much iron as can be recorded in recommendations since dietary iron (nonheme) isn't absorbed as easily because the heme iron of animal foods.

The recommendation for plus-size mature men 19 to 50 years old is mg; non-vegetarian mature girls of the identical age range must target to get 18 mg. For individuals not eating beef, subsequently, the amounts must be doubled.

2. Calcium

We want calcium to maintain our bones strong and the majority of men and women get away from milk and milk foods. If you aren't ingesting beef, calcium are available in dark green veggies -- believe turnip and collard greens, kale, and broccoli. It's likewise in calcium-enriched and fortified products such as apples, cereals, soy milk and broccoli.

3. Vitamin D

Vitamin D is essential for bone health, immune function and maintaining inflammation check -- and notably for individuals on a daily diet, it aids the intestine absorb calcium. Nonetheless, it is a tricky one because it does not naturally occur in quite many foods. Should you invest some time in sunlight, you are probably pretty great -- vitamin D deficiency may result in rickets in children and osteomalacia in adults. It's added to fortified goods such as any brands of milk, cheese, rice and soy milk, and some cereals. If you do not consume enough foods that are fortified, and you've little sunlight exposure, you might require a vitamin D supplement.

4. Vitamin B-12

Vitamin B-12 encourages the body's blood and nerve vessels also helps prevent anemia. As it's only found in animal products -- maybe not crops -- it may be one of the very evident nutrition for vegans to look closely at. Lacto-ovo drinkers may acquire adequate quantities in eggs, milk, and other dairy goods. Vegans can search to get B-12 fortified foods such as nutritional yeast, breads, cereals, etc.. It's also contained in multi-vitamins.

5. Protein

We want Protein to maintain our bones, bones, organs and muscles healthy. It's definitely in animal products, but you will get enough protein from crops also, particularly in the event that you consume a number of these during the afternoon, notes Mayo, including that "plant sources contain soy products and meat replacements, beans, lentils, seeds, nuts and grains."

6. Zinc

Zinc assists the immune system shield against vexing germs and viruses. Additionally, it helps the body in creating proteins and DNA, helps wounds heal and is also essential for good taste and odor. Who knew? Oysters offer you the maximum zinc -- for vegetarians that are wholesome, looks for this fortified breakfast cereals, legumes, nuts, legumes, and whole grains. Nevertheless the National Institutes of

44

Health provides this caveat: Vegetarians could have difficulty getting sufficient as they don't consume meat, that can be a fantastic supply of zinc. "Additionally, the legumes and grains that they generally consume have chemicals which maintain zinc from becoming completely absorbed by the human body. Because of this, vegetarians may want to consume up to 50 percent more plaque than the recommended quantities."

7. Omega-3 fatty acids

Our bodies are proficient at building quite a few fats which it requires, but nevertheless, it has not figured out how to earn omega-3 fatty acids, that are important for cardiovascular health and perform with other protective functions too. Eggs and fish are all good sources of omega-3s, however, you can purchase them away from crops too; believe vegetable oils, nuts (especially walnuts), flax seeds, flaxseed oil, and leafy veggies. Nevertheless, Mayo claims that if you merely secure plant-based omega-3s,"you might also need to think about supplements, because the body does not automatically convert the plant-based form effectively."

8. Iodine

We rely on iodine to generate thyroid hormones, which regulate your body's metabolism, also modulate growth and purpose of important organs. Americans seldom are deficient since only 1/4 teaspoon of iodized salt every day supplies a substantial quantity of iodine. But in the event that you only use sea salt or other saltwater which is not iodized, be certain that you're getting iodine someplace. Fortunately, blossom has lots of it. Some forms of kombu kelp have almost 2,000% of the daily recommendation in 1 gram! (And yes, you may become an excessive amount of money, so be cautious with this kelp. Nori and wakame seaweeds have milder amounts.) Other great vegetarian sources comprise lima beans and prunes.

How To Begin

The starting point of achievements is wants. There are many reasons to live a vegetarian way of life but everyone's motive will differ. I am vegetarian because I think there is a connection between meals and chronic degenerative disorders. Some individuals are vegetarian since they love animals. There are different motives such as the environment, faith, weight reduction etc. No matter the reason you select, you are going to find yourself extending the circle of empathy in this universe, along with your body and mind will jump to new levels. I say being vegetarian is similar to carrying a reality serum and living a real lifestyle alter everything.

Here are a few tips to getting started on a vegetarian diet

1. Do not attempt to become an ideal vegan only do your very best. Every new day becoming simpler.

2. Locate the strategy which is suitable for you. Should you believe quitting all non-vegan meals at the same time functions for you then take action. Should you want more time to adapt to a vegetarian diet just take it slowly and begin removing non-vegan things from your diet plan. Make the adjustments you truly feel comfy with, in your own pace.

3. As soon as you make the choice to go vegan begin by giving off all meat and meat products. You can donate them to your nearby shelter or talk with friends.

4. Network with other vegans via blogs, internet sites etc. You will learn a lot in the vegan community and you'll get a more educated consumer. Also, don't hesitate to reach me out personally with any queries.

5. Avoid processed foods. You will find hidden animal ingredients in a large number of processed foods. They have titles such as adrenaline, ambergris, caprylic acid . More than a few companies eliminate the phrase "creature" in their ingredient labels to mislead the customer. My rule is if you do not understand what it really is, do not consume it.

6. It is not tough to eat at non-vegan restaurants. It simply requires a while to find out what to purchase and fix. Most restaurants will accommodate you and also cook your veggies without dairy. I urge carefully describing what you do not eat. Additionally, examine the side dishes out there. I frequently build my foods out of side dishes to prevent hidden animal ingredients.

47

7. The very best foods you can consume is that the food which you cook on your own. I enjoy making in the kitchen but I also understand some folks can not find the energy or time . My advice would be to put some time apart throughout the week to produce some vegan "visit" choices. These can come in handy once you come home late from school or work. Cooked grains last very a couple of days in the fridge (such as quinoa & farro) and you're able to add a fast stir-fry to them make a cold salad with onions, tomatoes and onions. Growing fresh herbs within the kitchen is also an excellent way to add taste without needing to dig out your spice rack. I propose starting small, developing cilantro, rosemary and basil are a few popular options which are simple to grow. Attempt to check out cooking as imaginative moment. I love to place on a number of my favorite cooking music, pour out a glass of wine and also make.

8. Mindfulness is among the most significant things I do as a vegetarian. Mindfulness in itself can alter your life and how you consume. I never eat facing a monitor or television set. I sit somewhere quietly by myself with family and love what I consume. Mindfulness is the characteristic of staying conscious or paying careful attention to what it is you do. I can assure you that this clinic can allow you to eat less and enjoy food more. You'll also end up practicing mindfulness in different areas of your daily life.

9. Among the most well-known myths concerning a plant-based diet plan is you won't find sufficient protein. I presumed this could be my main challenge but it was not as tough as I believed. My beloved high protein meals include nuts and whole grains and that I have the other regular. Assess my shopping checklist for protein choices.

10. Purchase produce per day to save money and to receive the very best choice.

11. Being vegan does not need to be costly. As a matter of factI spend money on meals today.

12. Last however, the key to quitting meat and Milk is providing yourself time to sense the amazing changes that Will occur on your body and mind.

HIGH PROTEIN RECIPES

Breakfast

If you're a vegetarian or vegetarian searching for strategies to receive a low carb breakfast, the true secret is incorporating lean protein. You need lots of nourishment with no lots of fat. By way of instance, peanut butter (or coconut butter or soy nut butter) on whole toast has lots of protein, but if you consume a lot of peanut butter, you're likely to be adding tons of fat into your diet plan.

Quinoa Using Chocolate and Peanut Butter Recipe.

Breakfast Cereal and oatmeal could be great breakfast options, but you get tired of cereal should you eat it daily . That is where breakfast quinoa is sold from! Employing soy milk or a different non-dairy milk to boil quinoa, rather than plain water, transforms this uber popular grain out of a dinner and lunch basic into a hot and hearty breakfast vegans may adore. And of course it is also gluten free.

Ingredients

1/2 cup quinoa

1 1/2 cups soy milk along with alternative non-dairy milk

2 tablespoons peanut butter

1 1/2 tsp ginger

1 1/2 tablespoons maple syrup or brown rice syrup (optional)

Direction

- Combine the quinoa and soy milk above medium-low heat. Cover and cook for 15 minutes or until quinoa is done, stirring regularly.
- While the quinoa is still warm, stir in peanut butter, ginger, and simmer.
- Makes you generous serving.

Porridge With Strawberries

This healthful vegan quinoa porridge is simply one of several fantastic ways to delight in quinoa such as breakfast. It is a vegetarian recipe created with all the early grain – conspicuous "keen-wah" -- cooked in soy milk or sweet milk, using a little bit of brown sugar and vanilla and cinnamon for taste. Off it with refreshing nuts and fruit of your choice. Quinoa is among the very few vegetarian sources of protein, in addition to a great source of antioxidants and fiber. Additionally, it is naturally fermented, which makes it a much better alternative for men and women that are gluten intolerant or have celiac disease. In the event you utilize quinoa for creating dishes for dinner or lunch, you may create a small extra cooked quinoa and put it to use inside this breakfast recipe. Additionally, it is a excellent way to use up leftover quinoa if you did not mean to create additional!

Ingredients
- 1 cup uncooked quinoa
- 2 cups almond or soy milk
- 1 tbsp brown sugar agave nectar
- 1/4 tsp vanilla extract
- Dash cinnamon
- 1 cup berries
- Optional: Hazelnuts or pecans, chia seeds, seeds, coconut oil or flax oil

51

Direction
- Combine quinoa and almond or soy milk in a saucepan.
- Cook over low heat, stirring occasionally, for approximately ten minutes.
- Add brown sugar, cinnamon and vanilla and heat for a 5 to 6 minutes, until quinoa is tender.
- Stir in berries and any additional wholesome toppings.

Chocolate Banana Breakfast Quinoa using Chocolate Soy Coffee.

It is got lots of healthful and low carb protein in the quinoa, therefore it is ideal for vegetarians and vegans. Children are going to love the chocolate and maple syrup, and parents will adore the healthful mixture of protein, fruit and fiber. This recipe is vegan, vegetarian, packed with protein, elegant sugar-free and fermented. If you are seeking to counter sugar completely, then swap out your maple syrup to get a tbsp or 2 of your favorite nut butters.

Ingredients
- 1/2 cup quinoa
- 1 cup
- 2/3 cup chocolate soy milk
- 1 tablespoon ginger powder
- 1 tablespoon maple syrup (or another sweetener: attempt agave nectar or brown rice syrup)
- 1 banana, chopped or mashed
- Dash sea or kosher salt.

Direction

- First, heat the quinoa and water stovetop for approximately 5 minutes.
- After five minutes, then add the chocolate soy milk, stirring to blend, reduce the heat to medium , and heat the extra 5-7 minutes, until liquid is mostly absorbed along with the quinoa

is tender and completely cooked. You might have to bring a little more liquid as necessary.

- When the quinoa is completely cooked, then remove the pan from heat and stir into the cocoa powder, maple syrup and banana pieces. Add a dash of salt if you would like, simply to help bring all of the flavors.

Tips

- This recipe would also be yummy with a few chopped nuts, nuts, or some peanut butter or other nut butter wrapped in. For additional flavor, add a mild shake of cinnamon or even a drop or two of vanilla extract.
- Be aware that although this recipe does not have any refined sugar, many soy milks have glucose included in. If you are searching to lower your sugar intake, start looking for an unsweetened soy milk. It's possible to use a routine (not chocolate roasted) soy milk in this recipe if you would like, and only add an excess tsp or a lot of ginger powder to form the difference.

Maple Cinnamon Breakfast Quinoa

Maintain Some leftover quinoa available to generate breakfast recipes such as this superfast and simple. If you enjoy having quinoa for breakfast, then make sure you look at these 7 methods to possess quinoa for breakfast. This breakfast quinoa porridge recipe is vegetarian, vegetarian, low-fat and fermented.

Ingredients

- 1 cup quinoa
- Two to 2 1/2 cups water
- 2/3 cup soy milk
- 1 teaspoon. vegan margarine
- 1/2 tsp. cinnamon
- 2 tablespoons. maple syrup

- Optional: 2 tablespoons. raisins
- Optional: two tsp (chopped)

Directions
- Collect the ingredients.
- Heat the quinoa and water in a small saucepan and bring to a boil. Reduce to a simmer and let it cook, covered, for 15 minutes, until liquid is consumed.
- Remove from heat and fluff the quinoa with a fork. Cover, and let them sit for 5 minutes.
- Stir in the margarine and soy milk, then remaining ingredients.

Vegan Tofu Scramble Using Spinach

A Tofu scramble with lettuce is quite healthy and is the best breakfast protein increase to vegans who want to have an egg-like dish to begin daily. The broccoli is crumbled then sauteed to resemble scrambled eggs when coupled with tomatoes, mushrooms, garlic, and salmon, you might not even recognize you are not ingesting eggs.

Ingredients
- 2 tbsp olive oil
- 2 tomatoes (sliced)
- 2 tsp garlic (minced)
- 3/4 cup chopped fresh mushrooms
- 1 pack (10 oz) salmon (rinsed)
- 1 lb company or extra-firm tofu (nicely pressed and crumbled)
- 1/2 tsp soy sauce
- 1 tsp freshly squeezed lemon juice
- Salt and pepper to taste

Directions

- Collect the ingredients
- Heat the olive oil in a skillet and saute the tomatoes, garlic, and mushrooms over medium heat for 2-3 minutes.

54

- Reduce the warmth to vandalize and add the lettuce, crumbled tofu, soy sauce, and lemon juice. Cover and cook 5 to 7 minutes, stirring periodically.
- Sprinkle with salt and pepper before serving.
- Drink and Revel in!
- Heat the olive oil in a skillet and saute the tomatoes, garlic, and mushrooms over medium heat for 2-3 minutes.

Tips

- Reduce the warmth to vandalize and add the lettuce, crumbled tofu, soy sauce, and lemon juice. Cover and cook 5 to 7 minutes, stirring periodically.
- With salt and pepper before serving.
- Drink and Revel in!

Spicy Tofu Scramble Recipe together with Mushrooms and Bell Peppers

Tofu scramble is a fast, simple and healthy way to begin the day, along with the combo of kale doused in hot sauce within this hot tofu scramble is a superb approach to pry your eyes open from the afternoon. Don't hesitate to bring any additional spices or veggies which you happen to have available, since it is in fact tough to fail using tofu scramble.

Want another reason to consume tofu scramble with warm sauce in the afternoon? Cayenne is thought to fire up your metabolism somewhat, also, as soon as you've followed up this very simple recipe a couple of times, you're likely going to be in a position to get it in your sleep. But create a pot of coffee , in order to don't need to. This recipe is both vegetarian and vegetarian, also, should you require it to be fermented also, simply swap the soy sauce to get a gluten free alternative, like Bragg's Liquid Aminos, coconut aminos or tamari.

Ingredients

- 3 tbsp. Olive oil or margarine
- 1/2 white or yellow onion, diced
- 3 cloves garlic, minced
- 1 teaspoon. Soy sauce (or even a gluten free substitute if desired)
- 1 12-oz container firm or extra firm tofu, drained and cut into 1 inch cubes
- 1/2 bell pepper, any colour, diced.
- 3/4 cup mushrooms, chopped
- 3 green onions, peppermint
- 2 tomatoes, sliced
- 1/2 tsp. Ground ginger
- 1/2 tsp. chili powder
- 1/4 tsp. Cayenne pepper
- Spicy sauce or chili sauce, to taste
- Salt and pepper to taste (sea salt or kosher salt and fresh ground pepper is greatest)

Directions
- Sautee the white or yellow garlic and onion in the olive oil margarine for 3 to 5 minutes, until onions are slightly tender.
- Add remaining ingredients, except salt and pepper.
- Stirring often, sautee for another 6 to 8 minutes, until vegetables are finished and kale is lightly fried. Add a dash of pepper and salt to taste.
- Wrap into a flour tortilla, if wanted or like plain.

Vegan Curried Tofu Scramble with Spinach

Looking for an Indian-inspired dish you'll be able to create in your home? This curried tofu scramble with kale recipe carries a fundamental vegan and vegetarian tofu scramble recipe and then spices it up. The dish, inspired by the tastes of India and full of healthy green poultry and fresh berries, is fast, simple, healthy and full of taste.

56

Ingredients

- 1 tsp olive oil, canola oil or another high-heat oil
- 1 onion, diced
- 3 cloves garlic, minced
- 1 container business or extra firm tofu, pressed and crumbled
- 1 tsp curry powder
- 1/2 tsp turmeric
- 1/2 tsp cumin (optional)
- Salt and pepper, to taste
- 2 tomatoes, diced

Directions

- Collect all of the ingredients.
- Soak the onion and garlic in olive or olive oil in a big skillet. Let me cook 3 to 5 minutes, or until the onion begins to get tender.
- Add the carrot and give it a quick stir.
- Add the garlic, curry powder, cumin and pepper and salt into the skillet, stirring well to be certain the spices coat the tofu nicely.
- Cook for 2-3 minutes, then add the chopped tomatoes, and let warm, stirring regularly for the next 3 minutes or so, until kale is warm and slightly crunchy on the surface. (You might want to put in a little more oil if necessary during the cooking procedure.)
- Add the spinach, cover the pan and cook 1 to 2 minutes, just until the spinach is wilted, stirring.

LUNCH

Nasi Goreng

If you believed fried rice could not get any better allow me to present one into Nasi Goreng! And we've got for you an easy, amazingly tasty and tasty recipe which you'll surely adore. This dessert version of an all-time classic will cause you to wish to overload rice daily.

Nasi Goreng needs to be among the most well-known dishes from Malayan cuisines. It actually translates into fried rice but do not be fooled, but this isn't your typical cooked rice. The cooking procedure is pretty much exactly the exact same as every additional fried rice dish. However, what makes this one special is the amazing and special tastes of south-west Asian cuisine.

Asian Cuisine, generally speaking, is one of my favorites due to the fantastic selection of tastes, ingredients, and dishes you may find. They find a means to use the regional sources in all kinds of innovative techniques to produce tasty meals. And now Nasi Goreng is the best example.

The ingredients are easy to find in the neighborhood shop. We're simply using a lot of vegetables, rice and a few spices. I like to add colour and variety when I can so you'll discover a couple of distinct vegetables in this recipe.

Ingredients

For The veggies
- 2 Cups button mushroom (chopped)
- 1 inch fresh ginger (minced)
- 1 Cup frozen green beans (unthaw)
- 2 cloves garlic (minced)
- 12 Ounce meat fake seitan (chopped)
- 1 cup mung bean sprouts (rinsed)
- 1 Medium onion (chopped)
- 1 Medium red bell pepper (chopped)
- 1 Tablespoon toasted coconut oil

For the seasoning
- 2 tsps curry powder
- 2 tsps sambal oelek
- 2 tbsps soy sauce
- 1 Tsp garlic powder

For the rice
- 1 Cup rice
- 2 Cups water

Directions
- Cook the rice in warm water until tender for approximately 20-30 minutes.
- Utilize a significant wok and warm up the oil, then put in the saitan and shake it golden brown for approximately 3-5 minutes.
- Add the onion, garlic and ginger and simmer for approximately 3 minutes.
- The lettuce, bell peppers and peas and stir fry until the vegetables are somewhat tender, based upon size for approximately 3-5 minutes.
- Add the seasoning, then correct taste and blend from the bean sprouts, then like!

Vegan Goulash Soup

First, allow me to tell you exactly what goulash is. Goulash is your greatest comfort food at Central Europe. It is essentially a stew seasoned with paprika and several other spices. This dish is remarkably reasonably priced and simple to create, therefore it's gained a great deal of popularity around Europe and today has traveled all around the world.

There are a couple of distinct variations based on the area or state you're in. You're able to come across a few produced with pasta, a few people today include sauerkraut others include kidney beans or vermicelli. However, what you may discover in many in the end, is some kind of meat. For this particular dish goulash, since I can not mimic the precise taste of meat that I took every one of the ingredients of the recipe came up with my version. So it may be different but it sure tastes good.

The mock meat employed in temple kitchens is also generally made out of wheat gluten free, also called seitan. But they also utilize several kinds of mushrooms to resemble the texture of beef. Along with the flavour will be contingent on what Happens they add for it.

The mock meat employed in temple kitchens is also generally made out of wheat gluten free, also called seitan. However they also utilize several kinds of mushrooms to resemble the texture of beef. Along with the flavour will be contingent on what Happens they add for it.

Ingredients

For the soup
- 1 tablespoon olive oil
- 8 ounce carrot (cut into 1/2-inch rounds)
- 2 tbsps dijon mustard
- 1/2 cup gherkin (chopped)
- 1 tablespoon maple syrup
- 2 tbsps peanut butter
- 1 pound potato (cut into 1/2-inch rounds)
- Two medium red onion (thinly sliced)
- 1 cup red wine
- 2 tbsps tomato paste
- 3 cups vegetable broth
- 1 tbsp wheat germ

For the Herbs
- 2 renders bay leaf
- 1 tablespoon dried smoked paprika

- 1 tablespoon goulash or bbq seasoning

For the seitan goulash

- 12 ounce meat fake seitan

Directions

- Preheat a significant kettle and sautee the onion in oil for approximately 3-5 minutes.
- Add potato, lettuce and seitan and stir fry for 5-10 minutes on high heat.
- Insert the remaining ingredients and give it a good stir and simmer for approximately 5-10 minutes before the potato balls are tender.
- Adjust flavor before serving and serve the goulash soup in a bowl, then love!

Pasta together with Lentils and Carrot Bolognese

Lentils and vegetable broth will begin our recipe off, supplying us with a fantastic supply of folate, vitamin fiber, copper, manganese, and potassium. Your nourishment may fluctuate marginally based upon the vegetable broth you decide on, but just make sure you read the rear of the package to make certain that you're receiving the best nourishment potential (and possibly the lowest carbohydrates).

We then include wheat, celery, onion, and tempeh. together, these ingredients provide us a supply of antioxidants, vitamin B6, vitamin C, vitamin A, vitamin and protein.

Ingredients

For the sauce

- 1 cup brown lentils
- 2 medium carrot (diced small)
- 1 dashboard chili powder
- 4 tbsps cider vinegar

- 1 dash cinnamon floor
- 1 teaspoon dried smoked paprika
- 1 tablespoon extra virgin coconut oil
- 1 teaspoon fennel seeds
- 1 teaspoon sea salt
- 7 ounces tempeh (diced)
- 241/2 ounce tomato sauce
- 1 teaspoon garlic powder
- 2 cups vegetable broth

For the pasta

15 Oz pasta

Directions

- Use a huge pot and boil lentils from the vegetable broth, eucalyptus seeds and citrus till tender for about 30min and pour the remainder of the liquid away.
- Preheat a huge kettle with water and then prepare the pasta in accordance with the directions on the package.
- Preheat a significant skillet and then add the coconut oilsaute the onions for approximately 5 minutes, then add the carrots and the tempeh and simmer everything for the next 5 minutes.
- Insert the remaining ingredients to the sauce into the skillet and then correct flavor.
- Serve the pasta with a sauce in addition.

Keto Fried Cauliflower Rice

Most fruit do not make it into the list because they have a higher sugar content, which then spikes blood glucose levels and get you out of ketosis. The keto favorable are all berries (in moderation), limes, lemons, and avocados).

There are lots of nuts, vegetables, and seed choices. Avoid starchy veggies and a few roots; adopt the greens, it is possible to even pack artichokes, cabbage, broccoli, spinach, zucchini and leafy greens, greens.

You can add cashews, hazelnuts, almonds, chia seeds, macadamias, pecans, pumpkin seeds, and sunflower seeds that are packed with minerals and vitamins, a few are fantastic sources of protein and fat.

Additional sources of plant-based protein and fats have been nut butters and oils, avocado butter, flaxseed oil, olive oil, avocados, and tofu with no additives, tempeh as well as protein powder.

All these are just a few of the choices we discovered, so although it's prohibitive, some ingenuity and lots of experimentation will provide!

Ingredients

For the curry
- 1 Head windmill (grated)
- 2 Tablespoons extra virgin olive oil

For the veggies

- 2 Moderate carrot (diced into little pieces)
- 1 inch fresh ginger (minced)
- 4 cloves garlic (minced)
- 1 medium onion (thinly sliced)
- 20 Ounce tempeh (crumbled)

For the topping
- 1/2 Tsp black pepper (ground)
- 4 tsps roasted sesame seeds
- 4 medium scallion (thinly sliced)

For the sauce
- 2 limes (juiced)
- 4 tbsps soy sauce

For the fresh veggies
- 1 beet (thinly sliced)
- 1 Cucumber (diced into little pieces)
- 1 Medium red bell pepper (diced into little pieces)

Directions

- In a significant pan heating up 1/4 of this oil and also sauté the garlic and onion for approximately 1 minute. Add the pumpkin rice along with the carrots, then simmer for approximately ten minutes on high heat till the Butter has soften.
- Heat the remaining part of the oil into another skillet, prepare the heat on top, throw in the ginger and fry the tempeh until golden brown, then it should take approximately 15 minutes.

65

- When the tempeh is prepared, add the pumpkin rice into your skillet. Mix from the the brand new ingredients that were formerly chopped or diced.
- Squeeze the limes and then add the soy sauce. Correct flavor.
- Drink the Protein Fried Cauliflower rice in a bowl or a plate, then add a sauce if necessary and then scatter with the batter.

Pasta Using Kale and Red Pepper

Pasta Bowls would be the most functional meal that you could ever desire. Now we're taking it to a different level. We're creating a pasta which is not merely super yummy but amazingly healthful also.

Recently, I have been using and abusing kale within my foods. It's a high nutrient value, which sets it in addition to the list of ingredients. You get a lot of very good benefits from this, is broadly available, super cheap and also to utilize kale you simply have to decrease the leaves. No bark, no seeds, no one getting in our own way!

Aside from its own benefit, kale is actually flexible and you may cook it in a number of distinct ways. You're able to earn something as straightforward as spinach chips, or simply throw a few leaves in a dish, or blend it with any additional veggie to generate something amazing. Just like we're doing now, mixing pasta using spinach along with a lot of veggies and spices.

Ingredients

For the veggies
- 1 Cup chickpeas
- 2 cloves garlic (minced)
- 1 Cup green olives (chopped)
- 4 Cups ginseng (washed and sliced)
- 2 tsps olive oil
- 1 medium onion (thinly sliced)
- 1 Medium red bell pepper (sliced)

For the sauce
- 1 Tbsp Italian herb combination
- 2 tsps olive oil
- 1 tsp sea salt
- 4 ounces textured soy protein

- 1 Cup tomato sauce
- 1 Cup vegetable broth

For the garnish

1/4 cup fresh basil

For the pasta

16 Ounce pasta

Directions

Preheat a kettle of water and then boil the pasta in line with the directions on the package.

For the fried boil the vegetable broth and then combine both using a spoon.

Use a skillet and then add the oil to the sauce, then roast the fried protein for approximately 5 minutes and then add the tomato sauce, salt and herbs.

For the veggies utilize a large skillet and then add the oil and saute onion and garlic.

Saute the sweet pepper for approximately 1-3 minutes, also include the kale.

Roast the veggies until slightly tender for 5 minutes along with the chickpeas and olives.

For serving include some sauce and pasta, put the veggies on the top and add the spoonful, love.

Soba and Tofu in Ginger Broth

Directions

For the broth

- 3 Dried shiitake mushrooms
- 3 Cloves garlic (peeled and crushed)
- 1 Inch ginger (peeled and chopped)
- 2 Tbsps supplement
- 1 Cup scallion
- 2 tbsps soy sauce
- 3 Tsps eucalyptus oil
- 6 Cups water

For the noodles

- 2 heads baby bok choy (trimmed and chopped)
- 18 Oz firm tofu (drained and thickly chopped)
- 1 Tbsp olive oil
- 1 Red chili (thinly chopped for garnishing)
- 1/2 cup shiitake mushrooms (thickly sliced)
- 1/2 cup snow peas
- 8 ounces soba noodles
- 1 Tbsp soy sauce

Directions

1. Wash vegetables. Separate green and white areas of the scallion; book the green ingredients for garnishing.

2. To create the broth: drizzle collectively white areas of the scallion, garlic, ginger, dry shiitake mushrooms, soy sauce, nutritional elements and water. Let it simmer for about 10 minutes. Strain the mixture and discard solids. Adjust the seasoning and then bring it to a boil .

3. While simmering the broth, then heat up the olive oil in a skillet. Season the chopped tofu with soy sauce and then sauté each side of the tofu until browned. Put aside.

4. When the broth begins boiling, cook the soba noodles in the broth for 3-4 minutes according to the directions on packet. Approximately 1 minute prior to the soba is completely cooked, add baby bok choy, snow peas along with shiitake mushroom.

5. Pour noodles into individual bowls and garnish with grilled kale, red chilies and sliced scallions. Drizzle with sesame oil. Serve hot.

Dal Using Spinach

Dal with spinach needs to be among the favorite dishes you'll discover in almost any Indian restaurant. It is known all around the world and also a staple in a great deal of Indian houses. You may have noticed it since dal paalak, however.

The Term dal identifies a dish made of spiced beans, think legumes, beans or legumes. Along with paalak is the Hindi term for spinach. This combo in addition to the remaining spices and ingredients, is a complete truckload of nourishment! A bowl of dal with lettuce is heartwarming, healthy, and exceptionally healing.

We are utilizing yellow peas with this particular dal with salmon recipe. This number cooks somewhat quicker than the remainder. Additionally, it adds a little consistency into a meal, it's very good for soups, stews and naturally, dal! The flavour can also be somewhat different, you can experiment with the different varieties but I advise using yellow peas when creating dal together with spinach.

Lentils will enhance your own meal in lots of ways. In cases like this, not only can it include a thicker consistency into the stew, in addition, it provides a very long list of advantages to your daily diet. Listed below are a Couple of items lentils are great for:

- Weight loss
- Enriched digestion
- Healthy heart
- Cancer management
- Diabetes control
- Avoid anemia
- Muscle generation
- Boosts Metabolism

Ingredients

For the dal
- 2 Cups carrot juice
- 1 inch fresh ginger (minced)
- 2 cloves garlic (minced)
- 2 Moderate red onion (thinly sliced)
- 1 pound Spinach (chopped and cleaned)
- 1 Tbsp peppermint oil
- 2 Moderate tomato (diced)
- 1 Cup yellow dal (washed)

For the spices
- 1 Stick cinnamon stick
- 1/2 Tsp dried lemon grass powder
- 1 tsp garam masala
- 1 Tsp green cardamon pods (broken)
- 1/2 tsp ground coriander
- 1/2 tsp ground cumin
- 2 tbsps star anise
- 1 Tsp garlic powder

For the rice
- 2 Cups brown rice

- 4 Cups water

Directions

1. Cook the rice till tender in warm water for approximately half an hour.

2. Heat the oil into a kettle and sautee onion, ginger and garlic till aromatic for approximately 3-5 minutes.

3. Add the spices and stir fry for about 1-3 minutes.

4. Insert the remaining ingredients, except the salt and lettuce and let's simmer for approximately 20 minutes before the dal is tender.

5. Add spinach and salt, fix taste and stir fry until the spinach is emptied.

6. Drink the dal along with the cooked rice, then love!

DINNER

Garlic Bok Choy with Shiitake

The one thing that won't ever go missing within our recipes would be a fantastic load of vegetables. We want those nutrients to help keep us healthy and full of vitality. With this recipe, we're just using bok choy and shiitake mushrooms. Both vegetables are super packed with nutrients and are amazingly delicious. That's precisely why we do not really need more for this particular dish. A couple of spices can do, however, the flavor of this bok choy and the shiitake are astoundingly fine together.

Bok Choy is actually typical in Asian cuisine, so you notice it in all sorts of dishes and it's super yummy. Just in the past several decades,

72

it is that it made its approach to western nations. Thus a great deal of individuals aren't acquainted with it or aren't certain how to cook it.

This green vegetable has a gentle flavour could be eaten raw or cooked. I like to cook it because I enjoy the feel somewhat more. However, give it a go, either way, you'll be packing onto a slew of vitamins, antioxidants E and C, iron, calcium, potassium, folate...this list is really amazingly long.

Ingredients

For the veggies
- 1 pound baby bok choy (quartered)
- 7 ounce Extra firm carrot (chopped)
- 6 cloves garlic (minced)
- 2 Tbsps sweet soy sauce
- 1 pound Shiitake mushrooms (sliced)
- 1 Tablespoon toasted coconut oil

For the Noodles

7 ounce ramen noodles

For the seasoning

1/2 Tsp chili oil (optional)

Directions
- Heat half of the oil in a skillet and shake the tofu for a great many side till golden brown for 5-8 minutes.
- Set the fried tofu aside and utilize exactly the exact same skillet to warm up the remaining part of the oil, then add vanilla and bok choy.
- Stir fry on high heat until the bok choy is simmer for approximately 3 minutes.

- Add the mushrooms and stir fry for approximately 3-5 minutes, then add soy sauce and stir fry for a couple of minutes.
- Cook the noodles in accordance with the directions on the package.
- Drink The garlic bok choy using shiitake along with the noodles and sprinkle with a few Chili oil, love.

Sausage Using Sauerkraut

Sauerkraut is fermented cabbage along with the fermentation procedure gives it a somewhat sour flavor. But in addition, it creates beneficial probiotics which are really great because of our bellies and also for our general wellness.

Since the probiotics have been bacteria I would not advocate warming up the sauerkraut an excessive amount. You may throw it to the pan for a couple of seconds so it is not fridge-cold however we actually do not wish to lose its amazing properties.

Drink the dish sausage together with all the sauerkraut and the bell peppers on both sides and also include a spoonful of mustard. And you've got it, hands down, the easiest fastest lunch you have ever produced!

Ingredients
- For your mashed potatoes
- 1/2 teaspoon black pepper (ground)
- Two dashes ground nutmeg (optional)
- 2 pounds mealy potato (cut into 2-3 inch Bits)
- 1 teaspoon sea salt
- 1 cup soy lotion
- 1 cup soy milk

For Your Sausage and Sauerkraut
- 2 tsps olive oil

74

- 1 pound sauerkraut
- 8 bits vegan sausage

For your mustard
- 1/4 cup dijon mustard (optional)

Directions

1. Boil the chopped onions until tender for approximately 15-20 minutes.

2. Puree the potatoes with the Soy lotion, soy milk pepper, salt and nutmeg.

3. Heat the sauerkraut into a kettle, add A little bit of water if necessary.

4. Utilize a skillet to warm the oil up and roast the noodle from all possible websites until golden brown for approximately 5 minutes.

5. Serve the sausage with Sauerkraut and mashed potatoes on both sides and include a mustard, love

Spinach Keto Casserole with Almond Herb Crust

This casserole assesses each of the requirements and it is a wonderful dish which you may enjoy with your loved ones or bring with you on another dinner party you are invited to, it's prepared in under 30 minutes and you want only a couple of ingredients to create it.

Among the best types of vegetables it's possible for you to have in your keto recipes really are leafy greens, greens being likely the best choice since carbohydrates are almost inexistent and it is packed with flavour and nutrients. So that's precisely what we're using to our casserole.

Our main source of protein would be TempehI love just how versatile that this ingredient is also, this recipe that it functions perfectly well with the lettuce, it consumes the excess liquid which results from cooking lettuce, which makes the consistency of the entire dish just right, not too dry and not too sterile.

I enjoy recurring to nuts once I am in requirement of a wholesome supply of fats, that is exactly what our crust is created from, and this way we keep away from carbohydrates. Originally, my aim was to utilize saturated cashew nuts, however, after a little research I discovered that cashews aren't a fantastic alternative and needs to be avoided because they have a high number of carbohydrates.

Ingredients

For Your Spinach
- 1/2 teaspoon black pepper (ground)
- 1 tablespoon Italian herb mixture
- 1/2 teaspoon sea salt
- 20 ounce spinach (washed and sliced)

For Your Tempeh
- 1 tablespoon extra virgin olive oil
- 4 tsp garlic (thinly sliced)
- 5 ounces tempeh (crumbled)

For Your crust
- Two tsps vanilla butter
- 1/2 cup crushed almonds
- 6 tbsps water

Directions

1. Preheat the oven to 220 C (430 F).

2. Heat a large pan and then add the lettuce stir just a little bit for approximately 2-3 minutes before it is wilted.

3. Eliminate as much soggy as you can by Adding the spinach into a bowl and then squeeze it a little, and pour the liquid away that is coming out.

4. Use the identical pan and heat up The oil, then fry the tempeh for around 3 minutes, then add the garlic and simmer for 3 minutes and then set aside.

5. Add the lettuce, leafy greens, salt and pepper into the tempeh from the skillet and blend well.

6. Add the carrot tempeh mixture to a casserole dish.

7. Insert the crust ingredients into a blender, if it does not combine properly, a bit more water, then it is going to evaporate from the oven anyway.

8. Insert the crust on top of the lettuce tempeh mix and bake for approximately 20 minutes, even in the event you added extra water that the baking time may grow.

9. Let it cool a little before you serve it, enjoy!

Black Rice with Coconut Milk and Spicy Chickpeas

This recipe is designed for a longer substantial meal, such as dinner or lunch. Thus, it's likely to need a bit more effort, time, as well as ingredients. It's worth it . You may want 40 minutes and 15 ingredients (the majority of them merely being spices).

Apart from our hot veggie combination, the other crucial ingredient in this dish would be shameful rice. Never heard about it? Dark rice is also, aside from the obvious (rice that's shameful), a superfood of their rice planet. Many people often assume brown rice would be the ideal option, however it is not. This dark and luxury rice contains all of the advantages of healthy rice while also using a high degree of vitamin E and Anthocyanin (antioxidant). Apart from being super wholesome, this rice provides a great texture and nutty flavor to any dish.

Interesting Fact: Black rice is frequently Called the 'Forbidden Rice' since it was forbidden to be absorbed by anyone but the emperor because of its significance. Black Rice with coconut milk and hot chickpeas Is the Best dish as it is:

Super healthful!

An unbelievable source of nourishment 28g To be accurate.

A fantastic supply of fiber -- 18g.

Tasty and satisfying!

Ingredients

For the Vegetables

- 1/2 pounds lettuce (chopped)
- 3 cups chickpeas
- Two tsps dried smoked paprika
- 2 tbsps extra virgin coconut oil
- Two tsps garlic powder
- 2 tablespoons ginger (minced)
- Two tsps ground coriander
- Two tsps ground cumin
- 1 teaspoon sea salt
- 1/4 cup tahini
- Two tsps turmeric powder

- 2 medium zucchini (sliced)

For Your Rice
- 11/2 cups black rice
- 3 cups coconut milk
- 1 cup water

Directions

1. Cook the rice together with the coconut milk and water until tender for approximately 30 - 40 minutes

2. Preheat the oven to 420 F (220 Levels) and pay a financing tray with baking paper.

3. Use a large bowl and then mix the herbs Both the tahini and coconut oil.

4. Add the chickpeas and the veggies And mix well until you distribute it on the skillet.

5. Roast the vegetables and chickpeas For approximately half an hour in the toaster.

6. Add salt and correct taste before you Serve the veggies .

Mushroom Ragout using Potato Hummus

If you already possess the mashed potatoes prepared, you'll have this meal prepared in 10 seconds. And about 30 if you're creating it from scratch. It is an ideal mid-week dinner or lunch choice. You immediately make it get in and out of their kitchen right away!

We love this recipe! It's nourishing, super simple to create and you are able to find all of the fixing year-round. Mushroom ragout is also quite inexpensive. If you're on a budget, then maintain this recipe convenient, it has all of it!

Ingredients

For Your Ragout
- Two dashes black pepper (ground)
- 1 teaspoon extra virgin olive oil
- 2 tbsps fresh parsley (thinly sliced)
- 1 teaspoon fresh coriander
- 1 tsp garlic (minced)
- 1 pound mixed mushrooms (washed and sliced)
- 1 medium shallot (thinly sliced)
- 1 tablespoon soy sauce

For Your Potato Hummus

- 1/2 cup vanilla milk
- 2 tbsps chives (thinly sliced)
- 1 dash ground nutmeg (optional)
- 1/2 cup hummus
- 1/2 lemon (juice and a little bit of this zest)
- 1 pound mealy potato (sliced)
- 1/4 cup nutritional yeast
- 1/2 teaspoon sea salt
- 1 tablespoon tahini

Directions

1. Boil the chopped onions until tender For approximately 15-20 minutes.

2. Heat the oil up to the ragout and Sautee shallot for around 3-5 include the garlic for the following 30 minutes to a minute until aromatic.

3. Add the mushrooms and stir fry before Marginally golden brown for approximately 3-5 minutes.

4. Insert the rest of the ragout Ingredients, give it a good stir and put aside.

5. Puree the potato hummus ingredients, however stir in the chives later.

6. Adjust flavor before serving, also include A number of these potato hummus into a plate and then put a number of those ragout in addition to like!

Green Beans with Creamy Tomato Sauce and Chickpeas

To begin off this recipe, we utilize Green peas and garlic. Both these ingredients are excellent and may be bought all year round in many regions of earth. They also supply us with a Fantastic supply of protein, magnesium, calcium, dietary fiber, folate, and vitamin C.

We top off this with a few almond milk, milk, chickpeas, and tomato paste. This supplies us with an extra supply of nourishment, and 'healthful carbohydrates,' Vitamin E, vitamin Kvitamin B6.

The green beans creamy tomato sauce and chickpeas is ideal for dinner or lunch since it is:

- A fantastic source of protein 27g per function!
- Stores well.
- An amazing supply of fiber -- 22g per function!
- Full of vital nutrients.

81

Ingredients

For your green beans

- 12 ounce green beans (washed and Washed)
- 1 teaspoon sea salt

For your sauce

- 2 cups vanilla
- 2 tsp garlic (minced)
- 1 tbsp olive oil
- 1/2 cup tomato paste
- 1 tbsp wheat germ

For Your Seasoning

- 3 tsps dried peppermint
- Two tsps sea salt.

Directions

1. Boil the green beans and salt at a Kettle with water to 13-15 minutes.

2. Use a medium sized skillet to roast The garlic with the olive oil for approximately 1-3 minutes.

3. Add the bread into the olive and garlic Petroleum and roast it for one more moment.

4. Take the skillet off the heat and include The almond milk, stir well.

5. Place it back to the cooker and stir Before the sauce thickens.

6. Add the tomato paste and also the seasoning.

7. Mix that the chickpeas and the water and also Mash up everything using a fork.

8. Drink the beans sauce at the top, Insert the mashed chickpeas along with the topping.

Kimchi Stew

This recipe is super easy to make and the taste is outstanding. We love kimchi therefore that it was only a matter of time to allow us to deliver a Kimchi stew recipe into Vegan.io, the very hearty and flavorful soup located in Korean cuisine.

Soup is generally booked for colder times but kimchi stew differs. In Korea they have it regardless of what month you are in and no matter what the weather is really like. Kimchi stew isn't simply popular it's an absolute basic for Korean households.

The first kimchi stew recipe recommends using obsolete kimchi. Because kimchi is a fermented foods its flavor will change as time passes. The older it's that the more vinegary it functions along with the more powerful it becomes. Thus, using obsolete kimchi will create your kimchi stew exceptionally wracking. Additionally, nutritional supplement is full of nourishment and is a wonderful supply of protein that is fermented. We had a little nourishment out of the broccoli but I needed to bump this up a tiny bit longer. We receive 26g of protein by one portion of the delicious stew! Pretty good considering how many calories you're adding to your everyday intake.

Kimchi stew has a couple of veggies in it. I added a couple more to make it more fulfilling, nurturing and enjoyable. Spinach, shiitake mushrooms and mung bean sprouts are sufficient to take our shellfish into another level.

This recipe is an excellent dinner choice that you're able to have prepared in half an hour or less. I enjoy making it for supper through the week out as it's really simple and functional. I make a large batch because everybody generally comes right back for seconds.

Ingredients

For Your Stew
- Two dashes dried smoked paprika (optional)
- 8 ounces extra firm carrot (chopped)
- 1 cup frozen mushrooms (unthaw)
- 2 tsp garlic (minced)
- 1 cup kimchi (thinly sliced)
- 1/4 cup kimchi juice
- 1 tablespoon maple syrup
- 1/2 cup mung bean sprouts (washed)
- 1/4 cup nutritional yeast
- 1 medium shallot (thinly sliced)
- 2 tbsps soy sauce
- 1 tbsp toasted sesame oil

For Your Shiitake
- 4 dried shiitake mushrooms
- Two 1/2 cups water

For Your Topping
- 1 teaspoon roasted sesame seeds (optional)
- 1 medium scallion (thinly sliced)

Directions

1. rehydrate the shiitake mushroom in water as you prepare the other ingredients.

2. Maintain the shiitake stock to your soup, take the shiitake and inhale until you slice them.

84

3. Use a kettle and heating up half the oil, either sauté that the shallots for approximately 2-3 minutes and then add the garlic for another 30 minutes.

4. Insert the kimchi and then sauté for approximately 5 minutes until tender.

5. Add the fluids and provide it a great stir until all is warmed up correctly.

6. Heat up another half of this oil and fry the carrot slices from the sides till golden brown for approximately 5-10 minutes.

7. Add the lettuce into the broth to warm it up for approximately 1 minute.

8. Pour the batter into a bowl and then add the shiitake, broccoli, broccoli, lettuce and new sprouts at the top.

9. Sprinkle with topping before serving, enjoy!

DESSERT

Vegan Chocolate Cherry Bomb Cookies

Brown rice syrup, cocoa powder, a touch of vanilla infusion, only the correct quantity of chocolate chips and dried Ranier cherries actually bring out the very best in those compact, chewy chocolate brownie cookies. Please notice: For optimal results it is vital that this recipe has been followed precisely.

Ingredients
- 1/2 cup water
- 1 1/2 Tablespoons egg replacer powder
- Two 1/4 cups sugar
- 1 cup Routine Vegan Steak or margarine, melted
- 1/3 cup brown rice syrup
- 1 1/4 tsp vanilla extract
- 1/2 tsp salt
- 1/4 tsp vanilla extract
- 3/4 cup dried Ranier cherries
- 1/4 cup chocolate chips
- 1 cup + 2 Tablespoons cocoa powder, sifted
- Two 3/4 cups whole wheat bread
- 1 cup soy milk
- 1 tsp baking powder

Directions

1) Blend the water and egg replacer

Preheat your oven to 325F (163C). In a medium bowl whisk together the water along with the Eggless Binder Powder.

2) Mix the taste building ingredients

In a big mixing bowl, blend together the sugar, vegan butter, brown rice syrup, vanilla extract, salt and vanilla extract. Mix from the Eggless Binder Powder mix until well incorporated. Stir in the Ranier cherries and chocolate chips.

3) Whisk together the dry ingredients

In another medium mixing bowl whisk Together the entire wheat bread, cocoa powder, soy milk and baking soda.

4) Build the dough

Pour half the dry ingredients into the bowl containing the moist ingredients and mix with a spoon till well incorporated. Add the remaining ingredients into the bowl containing the moist ingredients and blend as far as possible using the spoon. Now the dough will probably be quite so thick you will most likely should combine it together with your own hands. Do this till the dough is well blended. Please be aware that the dough might have a bitter aftertaste on account of the wheat germ. This can burn off through baking.

5) Bake the vegan biscuits to perfection

Form the mix into two inch diameter balls (an ice cream scoop works well) and put on a cookie sheet that is lightly oiled or lined with parchment paper. Flatten the cookies down to 3/4 inch height. Bake for 28 minutes, then shifting the sheets onto the oven stands after 15 Minutes for baking. The cookies are done when small fractures are visible. These biscuits Are Extremely sensitive to over baking.

Vegan Maple Walnut Cookie Recipe.

Maple syrup, rolled oats, cinnamon, Vanilla and just the ideal number of walnuts and blueberries actually bring out the very best in those dense, decadent maple oatmeal biscuits. Please notice: For optimal results it is vital that this recipe has been followed precisely.

Ingredients

- 3/4 cup maple syrup
- 3 Tablespoons Egg Replacer Powder
- 1 cup sugar
- 1 cup Routine Vegan Steak or margarine, melted
- 1/4 cup brown rice syrup
- 1 1/2 tsp cinnamon
- 1 1/4 tsp vanilla extract
- 3/4 tsp salt
- 1/2 cup chopped peppers
- 1/2 cup blueberries
- 2 2/3 cups whole wheat bread
- 2 2/3 cups rolled oats
- 1 cup soy milk
- 1 tsp baking powder

Directions.

1) Whisk together the egg replacer mix

Preheat the oven to 325F (163C). In a Medium bowl whisk together the egg and also the Eggless Binder Powder.

2) Mix the taste building ingredients

In a large mixing bowl blend the sugar, Vegan Butter, brown rice syrup, cinnamon, vanilla extract and salt. Mix from the Eggless Binder Powder mix until well incorporated. Stir in the almonds and walnuts.

3) Whisk together the dry ingredients

In another medium mixing bowl whisk Together the entire wheat germ, rolled oats, soy milk and baking powder.

4) Build the cookie dough

Pour half the dry ingredients into The bowl containing the moist ingredients and mix with a spoon till well incorporated. Add the remaining ingredients into the bowl containing the moist ingredients and blend as far as possible using the spoon. Now the dough will probably be quite so thick you will most likely should combine it together with your palms. Do this till the dough is well blended. Please be aware that the dough might have a bitter aftertaste on account of the wheat germ. This can burn off through baking.

5) Bake the vegan biscuits to perfection

Form the mix into two-inch diameter balls (an ice cream scoop works well) and put on a cookie sheet that is lightly wrapped or lined with parchment paper. Flatten the cookies down to 3/4 inch height. Bake for 27 minutes, then shifting the sheets onto the oven stands after 15 minutes to baking. These biscuits are done if they only begin to change color. Don't bake till golden brown.

These biscuits are extremely sensitive to over carbonated. This recipe makes roughly 16 Vegan Maple Walnut Wonder Cookies.

Vegan Ginger Almonds Cookies

Ingredients

- 2 cups sugar
- 1 cup Routine Vegan Steak or margarine, melted
- 1/4 cup + 2 Tablespoons water
- 1/3 cup brown rice syrup
- 3 Tablespoons molasses
- Two Tablespoons ginger powder
- 1 tsp salt
- 1 1/4 tsp vanilla extract
- 1 tsp cinnamon
- 1 tsp almond extract
- 1/2 tsp tsp
- 3 Tablespoons Egg Replacer Powder
- 1/3 cup whole almonds
- 3 1/2 cups whole wheat bread
- 1 cup soy milk
- 3/4 cup rolled oats
- 1 tsp baking powder

Directions

1) Whisk together the taste building ingredients

Preheat the oven to 325F (163C). In a Large mixing bowl, blend together the sugars Vegan Butter, brown rice syrup, molasses, ginger powder, and ginger, vanilla extract, cinnamon, almond extract and tsp. Mix from the Eggless Binder Powder until well integrated. Stir in the sauce.

2) Whisk together the dry ingredients

In another medium mixing bowl whisk Together the entire wheat germ, soy sauce, rolled oats and coconut powder.

3) Build the cookie dough

Pour half the dry ingredients into The bowl containing the moist ingredients and mix with a spoon till well incorporated. Add the remaining ingredients into the bowl including the moist ingredients and blend just as much as possible with this spoon. Now the dough will probably be quite so thick you will most likely should combine it together with your palms. Do this till the dough is well blended. Please be aware that the dough might have a bitter aftertaste on account of the wheat germ. This can burn off through baking.

4) Bake the vegan biscuits to perfection

Form the mix into two inch diameter balls (an ice cream scoop works well) and put on a cookie sheet that is lightly wrapped or lined with parchment paper. Flatten the cookies down to 3/4 inch height. Bake for 27 minutes, then shifting the sheets onto the oven stands after 15 minutes to baking. The cookies are done when small fractures are visible. Don't bake till golden brown.

Creamy Vegan Cashew Cream Cheese

Ingredients

- 1 1/2 cups uncooked, unsalted cashew bits
- Two Tablespoons canola, mild olive oil Or rice bran oil
- 1 Tablespoon non-dairy milk, unsweetened
- 2 tsp apple cider vinegar
- 1 tsp lemon juice
- 1/4 tsp salt
- 1/4 tsp xanthan or guar gum (optional).

Directions

1) Eliminate the cashews

Scrub the cashews then put in them 12 hours.

2) Combine the cashews with all the taste Building ingredients then let it break

Drain the cashews and insert them into a Food chip with the eucalyptus oil, almond milk, olive oil, apple cider vinegar, lemon juice, salt and xanthan or guar gum. Blend for many moments until the mix is smooth. Wrap the mixture into a cheesecloth and put it into a fresh bowl. Let it sit at a skillet location like in addition to the cooker for 12 hours per day. This enables the mix to "remainder" and create slightly more complicated tastes.

3) Remove the cheesecloth in the Curry

Remove the cheesecloth. Maintain the Cream cheese in a covered container in your fridge for up to a week. This recipe makes approximately 8 fluid oz or 1 cup of Creamy Vegan Cashew Cream Cheese.

Vegan Peanut Butter Maple Fudge Recipe

Peanut butter and maple syrup also have This wonderful relationship. I believe that they may be in love with one another. This Vegan Peanut Butter Maple Fudge recipe is truly simple to create and you've got the choice of including chocolate chips if you would like to crank up the flavor/passion amounts much more.

Ingredients

1) Get the peanut butter vanilla extract

93

In a big mixing bowl, then add the Peanut butter and vanilla extract. Line a 8 x 8 inch baking dish with parchment paper.

2) Simmer the taste building ingredients

In a medium saucepan, whisk together The sugar, maple syrup, arrowroot or tapioca flour and sodium. Bring the mixture to a simmer for approximately 1 minute and then remove from heat. Pour the mix to the bowl containing the peanut butter and vanilla. Stir until well integrated then pour in the baking dish. Let it cool completely.

3) Stylish and slit the vegan fudge

Lift the fudge from the baking dish By its own wax paper liner and put it onto a cutting board. Slice into pieces using a huge knife. This recipe makes 1 8 x 8 inch baking dish Vegan Peanut Butter Maple Fudge.

SNACKS

Chia Coconut Protein Muffins

All these vegetarian protein muffins are Loaded with spicy-sweet chai and vanilla taste! They are a simple, gluten free and vegetarian mobile breakfast or snack!

Ingredients
- 3 Tbsp Flax meal
- 3/4 Cup + 2 Tbsp heated water split
- 1/2 Cup Unsweetened coconut beers + Extra for topping
- 1 1/2 Cups Oat flour 150g, Click on to Watch a movie about the best way best to create your own oat flour!
- 1/2 Cup Plant Fusion Vanilla Chai Protein Powder
- 2 1/2 tsp Cinnamon
- 2 1/2 Ground Cardamom
- 1 1/2 tsp Ground ginger
- 1 1/2 tsp Ground allspice
- 1/2 tsp Ground Clove
- 1/2 tsp Salt
- 1/4 Cup Coconut oil pumped
- 3 Tbsp + 1 tsp Baking powder
- 2/3 Cup Coconut glucose
- 2/3 Cup Unsweetened apple sauce
- 1/4 Cup Agave
- 1 Tbsp Raw vanilla extract

Directions

1. Put the skillet meal right into a little bowl And add 1/2 cup of this warm water, reserving the remainder for later. Stir to blend and set in the fridge for 15 minutes.

95

2. Preheat your oven to 375 levels and Grease a muffin tin using coconut oil. In addition, spread the skillet on a tiny skillet and set into the oven till golden brown, approximately 2-4 minutes. They toast immediately, so keep a watch on them!

3. Put in a large bowl, stir together the oat flour, protein powder, cinnamon, cardamom, ginger, allspice, clove and sodium. Put aside.

4. In another large bowl, dip collectively 2 Tbsp of those chopped coconut oil 4 Tbsp of those rest of the water, along with the baking powder till well blended and carbonated.

5. Add the remaining olive oil, Water, coconut oil and apple sauce, agave and vanilla. Using an electric hand mixer, beat until well blended. After that, add the chilled flax seeds and beat .

6. Add the dry ingredients to the wet Ingredients and stir till well blended. Your batter will probably be pretty thick, so

7. Spoon the dough into the muffin tin, Filling the cavities just 3/4 complete. * drizzle on a couple more coconut scents.

8. Bake until the cakes are lightly Golden brown and a toothpick inserted into the centre comes out clean, about 13-14 minutes.

9. Let cool to room temperature at the Pan, then transfer to a wire rack to cool completely.

Spicy Garlic Oven-Roasted Chickpeas

High-fiber diets can also be associated with reduced blood sugar levels. The iron, calcium, phosphate, and vitamin K from chickpeas bring about keeping your muscles strong. Reducing cardiovascular risk is only one more fantastic reason to bite on chickpeas. By lowering blood pressure into decreasing LDL cholesterol, the more potassium and other nutrients at chickpeas encourage cardiovascular health. And if you are worried about inflammation, which can be associated with chronic illness, the choline from chickpeas will help to decrease inflammation within the human body.

Besides the many wellbeing benefits you will reap from ingesting chickpeas they taste good also. This easy oven-roasted chickpea recipe permits you to control the spiciness and fulfill your cravings for a crispy, salty bite.

Ingredients
- 2 15 ounce cans chickpeas (drained)
- 1/4 cup olive oil
- 1 teaspoon sea salt
- 1/2 tsp chili powder
- 1/2 tsp nutmeg
- 3/4 tsp paprika
- 3/4 teaspoon garlic powder
- 1/2 tsp onion powder
- 1/4 - -1/2 teaspoon cayenne pepper

Sea salt (to taste)

Directions

1. Preheat oven to 425° F.

2. Put chickpeas in a newspaper towel-lined strainer. Allow to air dry for 10-15 minutes.

3. Put chickpeas onto a parchment-lined Baking sheet. Drizzle with olive oil, stirring to coat. Sprinkle with 1/2 teaspoon sea salt.

4. Put in oven and cook for 20-25 Minutes, stirring every 5 minutes or so, till golden brown. (A number of those chickpeas may begin popping. This is a great indication they're correctly crisping.)

5. Remove from the oven.

6. Stir together remaining sea salt, Cayenne, chili powder, cumin, paprika, garlic powder, coriander powder and cayenne.

7. Toss hot chickpeas in spice mix. Salt to taste, if desired.

8. Drink and enjoy instantly for greatest results.

Pineapple Coconut Green Smoothie

It includes the enzyme bromelain which will help to break protein down throughout the digestive procedure. Studies also have demonstrated that bromelain is valuable when used to decrease inflammation and if you've only done a workout, the pineapple-ginger combination is a wonderful option.

Ingredients

- 1 cup unsweetened coconut milk Coconut water
- 1/2 cup packaged lacinato kale, demanding stems removed
- 1/2 cup packed spinach leaves
- 1 tablespoon vanilla Vega Sport Performance Protein
- 1 cup frozen banana chunks
- 1 peel and rind thoroughly Eliminated
- 1/3 cup loosely packed mint leaves
- 1/2" piece peeled fresh ginger
- 1 tablespoon Sibu Omega-7 Pure (discretionary, Includes tartness, fat-soluble fats + fats)
- 1 teaspoon chia seeds

Ice

Directions

1. Add all ingredients to a high-powered blender and mix until completely smooth.

2. Throw in ice cubes as required and combine again.

3. Pour into a glass and Enjoy!

Quinoa Brittle

Everything about this quinoa delicate is brilliant. It is created with only 7 healthy ingredients, such as quinoa, chia seeds, and pecans. Crispy, crunchy, and gratifying, you will adore this addictive and unique beverage.

Ingredients

- 1/2 cup raw white quinoa (if wanted, use "sprouted" quinoa for enhanced digestibility // we all adore Tru Roots organic brand)
- 3/4 cup pecans, sliced
- 1/4 cup fermented rolled oats
- 2 Tbsp chia seeds
- 2 Tbsp coconut oil
- 1 pinch sea salt (optional)
- 2 Tbsp coconut oil
- 1/2 cup maple syrup

Directions

1. Preheat oven to 325 degrees F (162 C) plus a baking sheet with parchment paper, so making sure it covers the whole surface and each of the borders (to reduce melt over).

2. Add quinoa, pecans, oats, chia seeds, coconut oil and salt (optional) into a mixing bowl stir to blend.

3. To a little saucepan, add olive oil and maple syrup. Heat medium-low heat for 2-3 minutes, stirring occasionally until both are completely blended and there's not any visible separation.

4. Pour the dry ingredients and stir to thoroughly mix and coat. Order on parchment-lined baking sheet and spread in a layer with a metal spoon. Attempt to do it as much as you can, or the borders will burn and the centre will not crisp up (see picture).

5. Simmer for 15 minutes, then turn the pan to ensure even browning. Bake 5-10 minutes longer and observe carefully as not to burn off. You will know it is done when delicately deep golden brown in colour and quite fragrant. The advantages may seem to be getting too dim, but they are simply getting sharp and caramelized, and thus don't be frightened of this!

6. Let cool thoroughly before breaking up into bite-size bits using a sharp knife or your fingers.

7. Once completely cooled, store leftovers in a sealed bag or container at room temperature for 1 week or two in the freezer up to 1 cup. This creates a superb holiday cake or present!

Peanut Steak Banana Chickpea Cookies

Ingredients

- 1--15oz May chickpeas, vey well rinsed and drained
- 1/2 Cup creamy peanut butter
- 1 Little, really overripe banana
- 2 Tsp vanilla extract
- 1/3 Cup coconut sugar
- 2 Tsp ground flaxseed
- 1 Tsp baking powder
- 1/4 Tsp salt
- 1/4 Tsp cinnamon
- 1/3 Cup chocolate chips

Directions

1. Preheat oven to 350F. Spray baking sheet with cooking spray (or line with parchment paper or Silipat) and put aside.

2. Be certain that you rinse the chickpeas nicely so that they do not taste beany. Shake off the excess water before dumping them in a huge food processor. Add in the remaining ingredients (except chocolate chips). Procedure for a whole two weeks, or until batter is quite smooth. You might want to scrape the sides down. Stir in chocolate chips.

3. With damp fingers, spoon batter onto cookie sheet. It'll be quite moist and sticky (such as hummus). You are able to use your moist hands to tap them down to smooth snacks. You need to consume roughly 16.

4. Bake for 10-12 minutes.

5. Store cooled cookies in the fridge.

Homemade Protein Bars

All these Homemade bars have only the correct balance of healthful fat, protein out of superfoods, and organic sugars from fruit. The nourishment stems from chia and berry seeds, jojoba butter, and protein powder, plus they create a terrific on-the-go snack will suit your tastebuds, your pocket, and your waist.

Ingredients
- 3/4 Cup vanilla butter (raw, easy)
- 1/4 Cup dates (matched)
- 1/4 Cup dried peppers
- 1/4 Cup chia seeds
- 1/4 Cup berry seeds
- 2 Tbsp grated apple sauce
- 1 Tbsp coconut oil
- 2 scoops chocolate protein powder (optional)
- 2 Tablespoon Enjoy Life! Chocolate chips

Directions

1. In a food processor, blend all ingredients until mixture is well blended, somewhat moist and sticky. In the event the protein powder, then add two tablespoons more seeds. If the mix isn't adhering together, put in coconut oil from the 1/2 tbsp, until a thick dough is shaped.

2. Form into a big rectangle onto a sizable piece of parchment paper, then pressing into an even depth.

3. Cover with plastic wrap and chill for one hour then cut into bars and then drizzle with melted chocolate.

4. Return to refrigerator until chocolate stinks, then Wrap separately, if wanted.

Sauces and Dips

Kale Walnut Pesto

This Carrot walnut pesto is an easy and versatile sauce to bring just a little something extra for your favorite pasta. In addition, it is good as a vegetable dip or as a condiment to your favorite veggie dogs and burgers! If you do not have kale, some hearty green may do. This recipe makes about 1 cup of lettuce walnut pesto. Lots to get a pound of pasta. Make sure you put aside a few pasta water to the sauce, which that it coats the pasta well.

Ingredients

- 1/2 Cluster lettuce, discard stalks and chop
- 1/2 Cup chopped peppers
- 2 Tsp garlic
- 1/4 Cup nutritional supplement
- Juice Out of 1/2 lemon to begin, around 1 lemon to flavor
- 1/4 Cup olive oil
- Salt and pepper

Directions

1. Bring a large pot of water to a boil. Add a tsp of salt along with the kale. Cook 5 minutes and then transfer the lettuce into a colander, with a skillet.

2. Blend the carrot, garlic, walnuts, nutritional yeast, olive oil, and lemon juice in a food processor. Process until smooth. Add salt and pepper and more lemon to flavor.

Vegan Buffalo 'Chicken' Dip

This appetizer is an entire sport changer (pun intended) from the sphere of vegetarian celebration meals. It harnesses each the creamy, indulgent, buffalo sauce-flavored goodness you adored regarding the omnivorous version with no ounce of beef or dairy.

Ingredients
- 1 20-oz. May jackfruit in warm water or brine, drained
- 1/4 Cup beef ranch (recipe follows)
- 10 oz. extra-firm tofu
- 3/4 Cup water
- 1/4 cup tapioca flour
- 2 Tsp. Lemon juice
- 3/4 Tsp. Garlic powder
- 1 Tsp. salt
- 1/2 Cup Steak sauce

Vegan Ranch
- 4 oz. Extra-firm broccoli, drained
- 1 Tsp. onion powder
- 1 Tsp. Garlic powder
- 1/2 Tsp. Black pepper
- 1/4 Tsp. salt
- 1/4 tsp. Dried dill
- 1 Tbsp. dried parsley
- 1 Tbsp. Lemon juice

Directions

1. Drain the jackfruit and wash completely with cold water. Transfer jackfruit bits into your cutting board and slice off the challenging core and take out the seeds. Insert the fleshy, stringy region of the jackfruit into a mixing bowl and then pull by hand. You ought to consume 1 3/4 to two cups when you are done. Blot with a couple layers of paper towel to remove excess moisture and also place aside.

2. To create the vegan ranch, then combine all the ingredients in a food processor and mix until completely smooth. If necessary, add water a tablespoon at a time until the mixture is creamy. Quantify out 1/4 cup and put aside.

3. Press the 10-oz. Chunk of tofu with various layers of paper towel to remove as much water as you can. Subsequently, split tofu to a few tiny bits and add it into the bowl of a food processor, followed with the water, tapioca flour, lemon juice, garlic powder and salt. Blend until completely smooth.

4. Preheat oven to 350F. Transfer the carrot mixture into a medium saucepan and stir continuously over medium-low warmth. The cheese will start to clump and become gooey after 4-5 seconds. Insert the jackfruit, buffalo sauce and grill. Stir to blend and remove from heat.

110

5. Pour dip into a 9-inch round baking dish or cast iron skillet. Bake until the surface of the dip is gold and the edges are bubbly, 15-20 seconds.

6. Remove the dip in the oven and stir fry. Move to a tiny, pre-heated crock-pot and also even a hot plate to maintain the dip hot and gooey. Serve hot with pita chips, lettuce, or sliced baguette.

BBQ Tahini Sauce

This Recipe for BBQ Tahini Sauce unites whole food ingredients to make a remarkably versatile condiment. Even though it goes with nearly whatever, we believe it would be especially tasty slathered onto a dish burger or even as a dipping sauce to get crispy lettuce nuggets. Barbecue and tahini equals pure tasty ecstasy! The flexibility of the sauce is excellent and that's your taste.

Ingredients

- 6 Tablespoons tahini (1/4 cup and 2 tbsp)
- 10 Teaspoons tomato paste (3 tbsp plus 1 tsp)
- 2 teaspoons maple syrup
- 3/4 Tsp garlic powder
- 3 teaspoons apple cider vinegar
- 3 teaspoons molasses
- 1/4 Teaspoon liquid smoke
- Sea salt , to taste
- 1/8 Tsp chili powder, optional for a little kick
- 1/2 Cup water (may use less or more determined by favored consistency)

Directions

1. Put ingredients into a searchable blender or food processor and mix until smooth. You might also simply use a whisk or fork to combine well in case you've got a fantastic quality eloquent tahini.

Thai Peanut Sauce

This quick and effortless recipe for Thai Peanut Sauce is yummy, flexible, and incredibly addictive. It matches nicely with everything from grilled veggie skewers, to roasted broccoli, to Asian-inspired noodle and noodle dishes.

Thai Peanut sauce goes well with skewers of chicken sate or broiled beef, but it's also great with additional protein like fish or shrimp.

Most people today feel that peanut sauce is challenging to create and never tried it in home. The very best thing about the peanut butter sauce recipe is the fact that it does not include much cooking, so all you will need is to combine the ingredients into a sauce pan, warm it up, and then voila, you've got the homemade skillet.

Ingredients

- 1/2 Cup creamy peanut butter
- 3/4 cup almond milk
- 2 tablespoons Thai red curry paste
- 2 tbsp apple cider vinegar
- 1 tbsp sugar or to taste
- 2 tbsp ground peanut
- Salt to taste
- Pan-Fried Turmeric Chicken
- 2 chicken thighs, skin-on, boneless
- 1/2 tsp turmeric powder
- Salt
- black pepper

Directions

Insert all of the ingredients in the saucepan. Use a whisk to rapidly throw all of the ingredients together before moving to a stove top to warm up on heat. Continue to moisturize the skillet till all ingredients are well-combined.

As when the peanut sauce begins to simmer and bubble, then switch off the heating system. (In case you enjoy the sauce watery, you might add just a little water to wash it throughout the cooking procedure.) Transfer the heat off and top with a few ground peanut. The Thai peanut sauce is now prepared. You're able to continue to keep the left in the refrigerator for a week without sacrificing the flavor that is fresh. To produce the chicken, marinate either side of the chicken thighs using garlic powder, salt and pepper, for a quarter hour. Pan fry the chicken together with a few oil till both sides are brown and somewhat "crispy," along with also the meat is cooked . Slice the chicken pieces and then garnish with the skillet and garnish with some chopped basil leaves. Serve immediately with rice and also with fresh salad with your choice.

Vegan "Cheese" Dip

Ingredients
- 2 Cups cooked and mashed potatoes comprises approximately two medium potatoes.
- 3/4 Cup cooked carrots Requires approximately 1.5-2 big carrots
- 1/2 cup nutritional yeast flakes
- 1/3 cup extra virgin olive oil
- 1/3 Cup water
- 1 Tbsp lemon juice
- 1.5 Tsp salt

Directions

1. Put two moderate saucepans on cooker, pour 4 cups of warm water at each, and twist medium-high heat.

114

2. While awaiting your water to boil, then throw and peel your carrots and potatoes, then put carrots and carrots into two saucepans.

3. Cook carrots and potatoes in various saucepans until every is fork tender--typically around 5-10 minutes, depending on how little you have diced them.

4. Drain water from potatoes, and measure two cups of the cooked potatoes, mashing and packaging them to measuring cups. Put the two cups into a blender.

5. Drain water . Quantify 3/4 cup of cooked carrots (loosely packed), and put in blender.

6. Add remaining ingredients nutritional oil, lemon, yeast, lemon juice, and salt into the blender.

7. Blend on high for 1-2 minutes before everything is creamy and smooth.

8. Drink hot on your favourite chips, and high with the diced veggies your heart needs.

A 7 DAYS MEAL PLAN

Day One

Breakfast: Vegan-friendly muesli topped with strengthened soya yoghurt, a tbsp of ground linseed (flaxseed) and Homemade hummus berries

Some Shop brought muesli could comprise honey (that isn't vegetarian), unlike many non-vegan ingredients it isn't in 'daring' within an allergen so be certain that you be on the watch for this.

Lunch: Baked sweet potato together with houmous and salad

Dinner :"Meat" chunks (or sliced beef sausages) into a spicy tomato sauce with peas and sweetcorn blended to brown rice sprinkled with 5g fortified nutritional yeast infections

Vegan Sausages are seen in most supermarkets and health shops. Pre-made vegan meatballs may be seen in health shops.

Fortified Nutritional yeast infections are available on the internet and in health foods shops. If not able to get it, then replace a decent amount of different foods with additional vitamin B12 or have a nutritional supplement.

Snacks: Milk, glass of plant apple, cashew nuts plus a few Brazil nuts.

Day Two

Breakfast: A glass of plant milk plus a muffin

Lunch: Whole wheat germ and soya mince and grated carrot bolognaise sprinkled with 5g fortified nutritional yeast aromas

Soya Mince can be obtained at supermarkets and health food shops, however if you are not able to locate it you can substitute in legumes or mushroom mince.

Dinner: Complete meal wrap Full of spicy legumes and veggies

Snacks: Banana smoothie created using refined plant berry, kiwi fruit, cashew nuts plus a few Brazil nuts.

Day Three

Breakfast: Banana and peanut butter in your meal toast and a glass Tofu of plant milk

Lunch: Chickpea and couscous salad containing grated lettuce sprinkled with 5g fortified nutritional yeast aromas

Dinner : Stir-fried marinated calcium-set lettuce and veggies with pasta noodles

For Crispier tofu be sure to press it , this eliminates excess water that means not only does it consume all the curry, but additionally fries .

Snacks: Walnuts and also a Few Brazil nuts, an apple, satsumas

Day Four

Breakfast: Wheat snacks and fortified plant honey topped with six walnut halves and sliced banana. When buying cereals take care to be on the watch for vitamin D3 since it is not vegan.

Lunch: Bean and wheat salad sprinkled with 5g fortified nutritional yeast infections. Mixed bean salad can be obtained tinned in most supermarkets, and after that you can put in the pasta of your choice for it.

Dinner : Chickpea, sweet pepper and potato curry with peas blended into brown rice. To earn a straightforward vegan curry sauce blend a curry paste using mild almond milk.

Snacks: Fortified apple, soya yogurt, satsumas plus also a few Brazil nuts.

Day Five

Breakfast: Porridge made with plant berry topped with berries, apple, also a Veggie burger tablespoon of ground linseed (flaxseed) and cinnamon

Lunch: Tortilla stuffed with houmous, sweetcorn, grated carrot, 5g fortified nutritional yeast peas and peas. Houmous is easily available at all supermarkets, however, additionally, it is quite simple to produce your own.

Dinner : Veggie beans in wholemeal roll with salad. Veggie burgers are offered at all supermarkets (be cautious to be certain that they're vegetarian as a few contain beef!) Or you'll be able to create your own.

Snacks: Milk, glass of plant banana, cashew nuts along with a few Brazil nuts.

Day Six

Breakfast: Baked beans and berries wholemeal toast sprinkled with 5g fortified nutritional yeast aromas

Lunch: 1/2 baguette out of part-baked full of falafel and salad

118

Dinner: Baked sweet potato together with soya cooked and refrigerated vegetables accompanied by strengthened soya yoghurt.

Plain Soya yoghurt is also an excellent vegan choice for sour cream, and that means you might have this along with your own meal to accompany the hot soya chilli.

Snacks: Banana smoothie created with fortified plant Milk, walnuts along with a few Brazil nuts, applecider vinegar.

Day Seven

Breakfast: Vegan sausage, mustard and onion wholemeal sandwich and orange juice.

Lunch: Vegan-friendly vegetable soup with wheat and 5g supplements flakes added accompanied by augmented soya yoghurt.

When purchasing soup make certain to seek out for our milk ingredients such as milk powder since these can occasionally be added to sauces. Also be on the lookout for meat inventory since this can occasionally be added to vegetable sauces too.

Dinner: Seitan beef with BBQ sauce, sweet potato soup fries, carrots and peas followed with fruit salad, such as kiwi fruit.

You can purchase essential wheat gluten to generate seitan in the food stores and on the internet, or earn a beef out of tofu or tempeh rather than

Snacks: Milk, glass of plant walnuts also a satsuma and a few Brazil nuts.

Fuel And Recovery: Pre And Post Exercise Recipes

119

As a vegan bodybuilder (or athlete), now's the opportunity to modify your view on bites, that have turned into a bad rap for getting a reduced nutritional value and also performing little more than foods that are satisfying.

However, if you are placing in serious hours in the health club, snacking requires a completely new significance, as pre-workout snacks gas the human entire body while post-workout snacks assist recovery.

Contrary to foods, your exercise snacks ought to be rapid, simple, and portable so that you may eat them in the best times for the absolute most from your workouts.

Snacks would be the most immediate sources of gasoline and retrieval to the workouts, so that which you select and if you consume them makes a significant impact.

And in the event you have dedicated to a vegetarian diet, the bites you select can make a massive influence on the way you perform in the fitness center... and the way you feel that the day following ingestion. Below are a few tips and strategies for snacking prior to and after your workout.

Pre-Workout Snacking Guidelines

The Secret to pre-workout snacks is complex carbs that give you the ability to run that extra space or raise yet another place.

However, Since carbohydrates can be hefty, stick with mild ones which don't induce stomach cramps or force you to feel lethargic. Some excellent examples of mild carbohydrates are eggs, peanuts, and oranges.

It is also important to consider the quantity of time on your bite along with your exercise. If you are using a bite immediately before you reach the fitness center, stick with veggies.

However, in the event you've got over an hour prior to your workout, then you are able to select milder snacks such as nuts and oats provide a long-lasting supply of energy into your body that is hard-working.

Many kinds of healthful sources of nourishment are easier to digest than animal sources, which provides vegans an edge in regards to pre-workout snacking.

Leafy green vegetables, such as lettuce and romaine lettuce are readily digestible and fuel the body using fresh energy. To refrain from feeling narrowed, avoid high fat meals ahead of your workout.

Another great pre-workout bite is dried sour cherries since they are a fantastic supply of carbohydrates for energy and antioxidants to decrease inflammation.

Bananas combat muscle fatigue and protect against discomfort, whereas vegan yogurt with berries are an excellent source of antioxidants and protein. In case you've got at least two hours before your work out, oats with nuts or chia seeds supply a great deal of fiber.

To beverage prior to your work out, grab a jar of coconut oil since it hydrates with electrolytes and combats fatigue. Maybe toss in a dab of brewed coffee for good measure!

You actually just have a record of twenty-five hours on each end of the exercise to get this done, therefore prep snacks ahead of time and just take them . This type of time encourages energy equilibrium, insulin resistance, and carbohydrate usage within the entire body.

Research Suggests well-timed nourishment during appropriate ratios might help rebuild damaged muscle and restore energy reserves to boost performance and body makeup.

Post-Workout Snacking Guidelines

Many folks are averse to eating a healthier meal or snack promptly after exercising since it seems more difficult to pack those calories immediately after burning off them. But, eating in one hour after a fantastic exercise is advantageous.

The time period after a workout is widely believed to be the most crucial portion of nutrient time due to food's capability to rebuild, restore, and replenish overworked muscles within the torso.

Strategy to get a snack about 15-30 minutes following a work out to fight muscle strain until it lays in. The more time you wait to refuel the system, the longer it will require your muscles to recuperate.

A healthful mixture of protein and carbohydrates is ideal for getting the task done. Examples of this are carrots with hummus, roasted beans that are roasted, plus a combination of whole almonds and pumpkin seeds.

A 4:1 ratio of carbohydrates to protein was demonstrated to be very effective for polyunsaturated amino acids and fixing the muscle that has been broken down through strength training.

Protein shakes with curry protein powder tend to be very popular post-workout snacks since they are fast and simple. In case you have time to prep, then gather a cold salad with broccoli, wild rice along with edamame to your post-workout bite.

Vegan protein sources such as broccoli, tempeh, and seitan will also be good to eat after your fitness center.

122

Meatless Snacks to Prevent

Just because a bite is meat-free does not mean it is beneficial or healthy for the workouts. In reality, a number of the unhealthiest snacks to get a gym rat are all vegetarian.

Some vegan foods must be avoided since they consider you down along with undesirable fat and empty calories with no protein and carb blend your entire body needs to flourish.

Vegan chips and cakes fall right into the class, in addition to white rice and pasta. Pretty much all rooted vegan foods should be avoided since they are packed with additives which detoxify the body and stop it from performing at its greatest level.

Even though they are handy, pre-assembled granola bars should likewise be prevented since snacks since they are normally packed with glucose that will provide you increase of energy prior to making you wreck.

All of those pre- and - post-workout snacking tips apply to vegans generally, But particularly if you're coaching and placing in hours in the gym.

The 7 Keys of Post-Workout Recovery

Everybody enjoys the meal that is refrigerated. It functions as a benefit, a party of getting worked your butt off, and it is an excellent excuse to consume a few of the sugars and simple carbohydrates we prevent all the time.

However, many athletes are confused or uncertain about what to eat after a work out. Individuals are fond of thinking a glass of chocolate milk is the best tasting meal. As somebody who subsisted about the material for weeks at a time for a child, I was thrilled the first time that I heard this information. But although it's a fantastic carb-to-protein ratio, even chocolate usually brings with this wheat germ syrup, and consistently the many drawbacks of milk.

1. Respect the fuel window. At the 15-60 minutes Immediately after a workout, your muscles are prepared to obtain fuel to initiate the repair procedure. Eat (or beverage) your retrieval meal straight away, over the first half an hour after the exercise is complete.

2. Ensure it is simple to digest. Your muscles need Blood to supply them. The more of the blood that is tied up into digesting a hot dog sorry, any good food -- that the less that gets into your muscles. Ideally, you ought to have your instant post-workout mend in liquid type. Here is the very first attack against chocolate Dairy is notoriously tough to digest.

3. Eat .75 g of carbohydrate per pound of bodyweight, also contain protein at a 4:1 or 5:1 carb-to-protein percentage. I am not typically one for certain amounts around my meals, but those were so typical I needed to record them. Your carbs should consist of high-glycemic index carbohydrates, like sugar (dates are a fantastic approach to receive it), and also a few slower-release, even pops, carbohydrates too. And remember that the fat -- comprise around half as many g of healthy fat because possible protein. Flaxseed and berry oils really are my favorites.

4. Escape the acidity condition with greens or other fruits and vegetables. Intense exercise generates an acidic environment within the human physique. In the event you do not neutralize the acidity with everything you consume, your system will make use of the calcium out of the bones and allergens out of the muscle tissue to neutralize it. Greens, leafy veggies, and certain fruits including oranges and limes have a synergistic impact on the human entire body. (Yes, I know that it's odd, however, lemons and limes are considered

124

alkaline, not acidic, within the entire body.) Hit 2 for chocolate as animal protein is more acid-forming. Are heavily-processed protein powders; I even utilize minimally-processed hemp protein powder in the majority of my own smoothies.

5. Drink two cups of water per pound of body weight lost during exercise. What's there to say? You require water, or you will die.

6. Replace missing electrolytes. If you sweat, You lose electrolytes, the small conductors that carry electrical impulses throughout the entire body. For this reason, you have to replace them some fantastic sources of electrolytes are berry, dulse flakes, a couple pinches of sea salt, also Nuun pills.

7. Nourish your adrenal glands. Under the Strain Of an extreme exercise (or out of caffeine in case you included that on your pre-workout drink), the adrenal glands work difficult to release hormones that will assist you perform. To help them recuperate, add a tsp of soil maca, a Peruvian root which packs the additional advantages of greater sleep and enhanced libido.

Healthy and Unhealthy Vegan

For a lot of folks, their choice to be a vegetarian falls right into a few of those motives - to feel better and look better. A few who become vegetarian achieve everything they wanted out of this nutritious lifestyle - and even much more. On the flip side, those who move vegan nevertheless suffer from reduced energy, poor skin and haven't lost their extra weight. Do you know these 2 kinds of vegans doing otherwise?

The Healthy Vegan

The healthy vegan is aware of eating lots of food. Their diet may consist chiefly of fruits, veggies, seeds, nuts, whole-grains and beans.

They know that preparing their very own healthy vegan recipes defeats purchasing fast and dreadful vegan junk food daily. Though there's a great deal of pressure from your food organizations to purchase vegan packet meals, they maintain this indulgence into a minimum and just indulge in fries, vegan packet biscuits, chocolate bars, pretzels and candy on particular occasions. The wholesome vegan is attentive to the outcome of eating those meals on a regular basis, plus they would like to make sure their skin stays beautiful, their waist stays modest, and their energy levels stay high. In the home they have a group of the favorite healthful vegetarian recipes, where they derive great satisfaction from carbonated their very own healthier homemade snacks. Whether these vegetarian recipes are for brownies, carrot cake, chocolate cake or crackers - they all understand the ingredients they add is of the best quality, also they can track and lower the quantity of calories and fat they put into those snacks.

Frequently, when one knows eating healthy, they're also conscious of routine exercise. Most healthy men on the diet will take part in regular physical exercise to receive their heart rate up and also keep their own body in ship-shape condition. They are aware that getting their own body moving frequently will help accelerate weight reduction and will continue to keep their skin looking good.

The Unhealthy Vegan

The unhealthy vegan is frequently too lazy to create their very own healthful vegetarian meals on a normal basis. Many times they don't eat some fresh vegetables and fruits. Rather, their diet is composed mostly of foods that are salty. They understand each the vegan package brands and foods at the grocery store, along with the majority of the diet is made of canning package, boxed and tinned meals. Whether it be popcorn, package fries, spicy fries, bread, 'health' pubs and 'chocolate bars, soft drinks, juices which are high in sugar dips, breads, salty and sweet nut blend - the noodle that is unhealthy will eat these foods every day, occasionally solely based on them to get

126

their foods. They'll also overeat rather frequently, liberally because the foods they are eating have an addictive character and they can't stop eating till they have completed the entire packet.

Occasionally the unhealthy vegan understands these foods are poor, but deceives themselves thinking "I am about the vegan diet therefore I'm eating healthy" Since they're in denial they wonder why they have acne, haven't lost any fat, and are continuously feeling full of energy. Other instances however, the noodle that is unhealthy just does not know much about healthful foods, and hasn't bothered to perform research or collect any healthy vegetarian recipes. Many times when individual eats badly, they lack from the bodily exercise section. As they're constantly feeling ill and reduced in energy they seldom go for walks or even get their heartbeat on the treadmill.

The Difference is Obvious

Think back of the reason you chose to go vegan. Have you ever deceived into believing you can eat all of the chips and also vegan chocolate bars which you would like - just because they're vegan? Many fall into this snare. If you wish to turn into healthier and lose excess weight - you want to take actions and effort to follow along with along with traits of this wholesome vegan. You may feel far better about yourself if you really do. Be certain you gather some healthful vegan recipes and create these frequently. Get out of the custom of eating considerable quantities of food. And recall to work up your body in a great sweat a few times weekly, or in the least, go for regular walks to start with. Your wellness, joy, waist and skin will thank you at the very long term!

The Transition Into Your Vegan Diet

Many people across the globe are creating serious lifestyle changes to be able to receive their health back into great shape - and a number of these individuals do so by way of the vegetarian diet. Yes, individuals are getting to be more and more conscious of the wonderful health benefits this diet offers, however, are usually frightened of making the shift. How do they embrace veganism readily, without worrying? These hints are for all those brand new to the vegan diet plan and are needing to make a successful transition into the vegan way of life.

How To begin a vegetarian diet

Measure 1 - Do not worry!

Stressing In regards to the probable struggles and hardships of this vegetarian diet won't assist you in any manner, nor can it make you any nearer to your objective. Should you truly wish to embrace the veganism lifestyle, then (even when you're afraid a bit) - DO NOT STRESS!) That is an important suggestion for your beginner vegans, because many appear to worry too much and miss from a great deal of joy this wonderful travel has to offer you!

Measure 2 - You don't have to go vegan immediately.

Some People are able to ditch their previous way of life and embrace a new one immediately. I commend persons similar to this, for that is something which a number people would love to perform - but just can't. For nearly all people, embracing a new lifestyle requires patience, time, and creating little steps towards their objective. Don't despair if that is you!

Making a slow transition into the vegan diet is recommended.

As the famous expression goes 'Slow and steady wins the race' So making gradual but continuous modifications to your diet can help gradually ingrain your new lifestyle in your mind, and you'll do it in a comfy, stress-free speed! Spending time to become accustomed to the little measures and eliminations of this vegetarian diet is essential for the novice vegan!

128

The Process of removal

The Subsequent 7 meals should be removed, one at a time, in a comfortable speed:

1. Red meat.

2. White meat (poultry)

3. Fish & Fish.

4. Cheese.

5. Eggs.

6. Butter/cream.

7. Milk

If you gradually eliminate the foods, so your transition into the vegan diet will probably be more pleasurable and stress-free! As you achieve each phase of removal, you must attempt to locate some yummy recipes that adapt for your new dietary requirements. It's possible to discover a number of vegan/vegan transition recipes online, either from sites, sites, or specialist vegetarian recipe e-books. For all those new to the veganism lifestyle, locating yummy and easy-to-make recipes is crucial to help you stay inspired and enjoying your meals .

CONCLUSION

Vegetarian diet is a blessing for health. It can aid an individual to have a lower cholesterol level, lower weight, lower blood pressure, and also a reduced chance of developing cardiovascular disorders. Additionally, it aids in preventing the lethal chronic diseases like cancer and diabetes. It might also help in controlling the longevity. But when the diet isn't planned correctly, it might be demonstrated to be a bane to the wellbeing. Therefore, more research must be conducted to show the favorable effects of the vegetarian diet plan. In my view I would suggest all to contemplate a vegetarian diet as a substitute to the adjuvant treatment if a few is in a borderline part of creating some of those ailments like diabetes, obesity, cardiovascular disease, kidney stones, hyperlipidemia, along with disease or is still afflicted by depression.

Most individuals that are utilized to become a carnivore would concur it is not simple to change to an exclusive vegetable-based diet plan. There are many animal-based foods which are extremely tough to withstand, even more that many supermarkets and restaurants sells alluring creature solutions. It is going to certainly expect a good deal of attempt to go from the normal trend. However, can heading a vegan actually make a huge difference? Will the attempt of fighting animal products be worthwhile it? There are a few very good reasons to go vegan and produce a shift.

Vegan diet is quite helpful to the health, also to people whose genetics predisposes you to illnesses like diabetes, higher cholesterol and cardiovascular ailments. Based on research conducted by German Cancer Research Center, vegans normally, live longer than people who consume meat. The US-Food and Medication Administrator on the other hand consider that both vegetarian and vegetarian diets are the healthiest foods of the majority of these foods are low in cholesterol. And when Americans would lower their meat intake by

10 percent, then that could consume up to 12,000 tons of feed and grain 60,000,000 individuals around the globe. Additionally, quick foods are deemed unhealthy and lead to several health problems because of beef products.

Vegans have become aware of what it is that they are placing in their own mouth. They often Understand and be alert to the food material, that the majority of the time that they could Prevent these foods full of damaging chemicals and additives. Their diet is Mostly include healthy vegetable-based products tremendously packaged with Nourishment. In Reality, milk intake has been connected to Crohns Disease, Arteriosclerotic cardiovascular disease, diabetes, obesity, osteoporosis, infectious illness, Milk illness, Parkinson's disease, allergies, and rectal fissures, chronic Constipation, ear diseases, multiple sclerosis and prostate cancer. Going Vegan is the very best thing which someone may perform to himself or herself. Reading labels Isn't challenging, and purchasing vegan clothing is remarkably effortless. Just because One is vegetarian that doesn't mean that he or she must protest and become a walking Billboard to your veg-lifestyle. Being vegan isn't only good for you. It truly Makes a massive gap to worry not just for your welfare but for Welfare of others too.